P9-CMV-688

Luxury Designs for Apartment Living

Also by Barbara Taylor Bradford

MAKING SPACE GROW
DECORATING IDEAS FOR CASUAL LIVING
HOW TO SOLVE YOUR DECORATING PROBLEM
EASY STEPS TO SUCCESSFUL DECORATING
THE COMPLETE ENCYCLOPEDIA OF HOMEMAKING IDEAS

Fiction

A WOMAN OF SUBSTANCE

Barbara Taylor Bradford

Luxury Designs for Apartment Living

Doubleday & Company, Inc., Garden City, New York 1981

To Angelo Donghia of New York and John Siddeley of London—
dear friends and talented designers

ACKNOWLEDGMENTS

My grateful thanks to Ellen Stark and Pauline Delli Carpini for their research, hunting down of appropriate photographs, and general assistance with the book. I would also like to thank all the interior designers who supplied photographs and whose work stimulated so many of the ideas and discussions in the book.

Photographic credits appear at the end of the index.

Designed by LAURENCE ALEXANDER

Library of Congress Cataloging in Publication Data

Bradford, Barbara Taylor, 1933–
Luxury designs for apartment living.

Includes index.
1. Apartments. 2. Interior decoration.
I. Title.
NK2195.A6B7 747'.88314
ISBN: 0-385-12769-3
Library of Congress Catalog Card Number 77–16899

PRINTED IN THE UNITED STATES OF AMERICA
9 8 7 6 5 4 3 2

Contents

Luxury Designs for Apartment Living

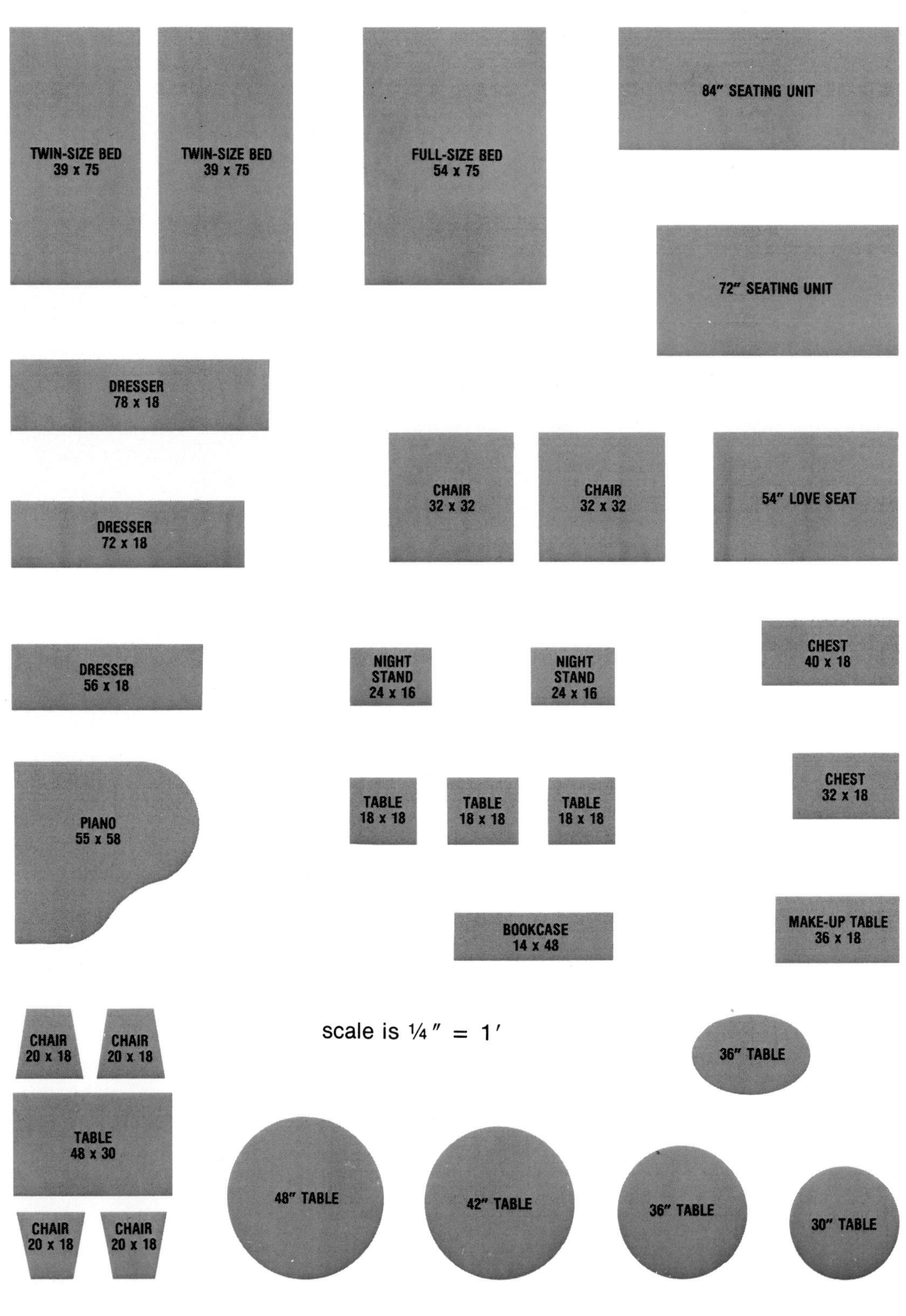
TWIN-SIZE BED 39 x 75
TWIN-SIZE BED 39 x 75
FULL-SIZE BED 54 x 75
84″ SEATING UNIT
72″ SEATING UNIT
DRESSER 78 x 18
CHAIR 32 x 32
CHAIR 32 x 32
54″ LOVE SEAT
DRESSER 72 x 18
DRESSER 56 x 18
NIGHT STAND 24 x 16
NIGHT STAND 24 x 16
CHEST 40 x 18
PIANO 55 x 58
TABLE 18 x 18
TABLE 18 x 18
TABLE 18 x 18
CHEST 32 x 18
BOOKCASE 14 x 48
MAKE-UP TABLE 36 x 18
CHAIR 20 x 18
CHAIR 20 x 18
scale is ¼″ = 1′
36″ TABLE
TABLE 48 x 30
CHAIR 20 x 18
CHAIR 20 x 18
48″ TABLE
42″ TABLE
36″ TABLE
30″ TABLE

1

How to Individualize Living Rooms

The living room is the hub of activity in an apartment. If it is to live up to its potential, it should have good looks and comfort, plus an individualized environment that says something about the occupants. This is especially so in a living room that is in a modern apartment of standard design, with room sizes and general layouts that are identical to all the other units in the building.

An expression of your personal taste in place of studied or copied effects helps to give this standard-type room—or any other room, for that matter—a distinctive and original appearance. There are many ways to express your tastes and, in so doing, create an individualized environment. For example, you can add a personal touch to a room through your choice of an overall decorative scheme that has distinction and pizzazz, one which lifts it out of the ordinary. The imaginative use of color does much for a standard room. A highly original look can be created through the use of a particular style of furniture, be it of modern or period design.

The newer and more flexible furniture arrangements enable you to bring individuality to a living room; incidentally, these newer ways to group furniture are particularly suited for today's more casual life-styles and are easy to live with as well. Accessories are a very personal example of your own taste, whether they be paintings, sculpture, or collections of objects. When these are used with skill and displayed with imagination, they add a touch of flair as well as highly decorative overtones.

However, before you consider all these elements and start making your choices, it's a good idea to make a floor plan. This is easy to do. Simply measure the length, width, and height of the room. You should also take down the dimensions of the windows and the doors. Use a piece of graph paper for your floor plan. Draw an outline of the room on the paper, using the scale of one-quarter inch to one foot or one-half inch to one foot, whichever you prefer. Indicate the position of the windows, doors, electrical outlets, radiators, and air conditioners—all these are important considerations when it comes to grouping furniture and accessories. This floor plan will assist you through all the various stages of decorating the room. It will show you how to get the most out of available space, help you to clarify your furniture needs, and tell you just how many pieces you can include. It will also help you when you start grouping your furniture, pinpointing the best arrangements for comfort, convenience, and good looks. A floor plan also enables you to take traffic lanes into account, which are vital in any room. Remember, people have to enter, leave, and move around within the room; they should be able to do so comfortably.

When you have completed your floor plan, go to an art-supply store and buy a template. This is a sheet of paper upon which are drawn the shapes of furniture, generally to a scale of one-quarter inch to one foot. Cut out the shapes and use them to make furniture groupings on the floor plan (see sample template).

Now you are ready to consider all those elements that help to bring individuality to a living room of standard design and stamp it as yours. Here is a breakdown of those elements.

Focal Points

Most living rooms of average design, particularly those in a modern high-rise apartment building, are without such traditional focal points as a fireplace, good windows overlooking a spectacular view, or some unique architectural elements. When this is the case, you must create your own focal point, since every room needs one to give it cohesion and a center of gravity. A focal point also acts like a magnet, indicating the proper areas for different furniture arrangements and creating a feeling of harmony and a balanced look within the room.

Begin by selecting an area within the room where a focal point can be created successfully. Generally, the largest wall is the most appropriate place for an eye-catching center of visual interest. After measuring the length and height of the wall, select the exact area where you will create your focal point. This will also help you later in working out furniture arrangements, traffic patterns, and the flow of the room. Your focal point should be of the correct size, scaled to the size of the room. For instance, a large room with a high ceiling and rather grand proportions needs a dominant focal point; a small room should not have a massive center of visual interest since this would overwhelm the room and throw it off balance.

There are numerous ideas for focal points. One of the easiest to create is a grouping of prints and pictures on a wall above a sofa. This is especially effective when the artworks are of different sizes and are enclosed in diverse frames. Remember that artworks should never be hung side by side at the same level. This creates a banal effect. Instead, hang the prints, paintings, graphics, or whatever you are using at different heights to create a sense of movement and life. Sometimes a really striking wallscape can be created when the art is interspersed with wall brackets containing pieces of sculpture or other decorative objects.

One large dominant painting or graphic looks most striking when flanked by handsome candelabra. Likewise, a period mirror can be most effective when used in the same way, especially when it reflects artworks on the opposite wall.

A freestanding piece of furniture can become a center of visual interest. For instance, a bookshelf unit filled with books, plants, and decorative accessories is most eye-catching. Alternatively, bookshelves built around a sofa work equally well. The shelves should be placed up the wall on each side of the sofa and then across the wall above it to ceiling level, forming a kind of alcove for the sofa. Again, a mingling of accessories and paintings among the books introduces a colorful and attractive look.

A wall covered with mirror tiles makes a lovely, shimmering backdrop for a glass table, or any other type of table, used to hold all manner of accessories. As a focal point this is difficult to top, as the expanse of mirror reflects images and objects in other parts of the room. It also introduces a three-dimensional look and expands the feeling of space through visual illusion. For this reason it is a good focal point for a small room.

A scenic strip of wallpaper or a mural can be used in the same way as a painting, or a group of paintings, to bring a wall into visual focus. Some scenes depicting gardens or the rolling, bucolic countryside introduce a three-dimensional effect, drawing the eye out as if to a space beyond. Various types of wallpaper reproducing murals are readily available today and are moderately priced. Many are easy to put in place since they are prepasted and pretrimmed.

Create an Individual Mood with Color

Color is a most effective decorating tool, doing much to give a room individuality. Before selecting a color scheme, consider the effect you want to create, the mood you want to produce, and also bear in mind that color can be most deceptive. For example, every color changes under different light conditions or when it is used in a small or large expanse; it can look brighter, darker, paler, or harsher and, of course, it can change the dimensions of the room completely. Here are some facts about color.

PALE COLORS

Any light color tends to recede, thereby giving the impression of pushing walls out and so making a room appear larger than it actually is. Pale colors such as white, beige, sky blue, apple green, daffodil yellow and other pastels reflect light and bounce it back into the room. They are also colors that introduce a lovely, soft, tranquil mood.

DARK COLORS

Colors that are either dark or very bright appear to advance into a room, creating a feeling of intimacy. They also tend to reduce the sense of space through visual illusion. Dark colors like brown, fir green, midnight blue, gray, red, orange, purple, and black all absorb light, seeming to produce a gloomy effect unless they are reinforced with plenty of artificial illumination. Some dark colors can introduce a tranquil note, while bright colors can often introduce a harsh look unless they are tempered with lots of accent colors to create a softening effect.

COLOR AND LIGHT

Color and light may be combined to create very special effects, some of which can be most pleasing while others are utterly dismaying. Color is capricious at the best of times, but especially so under changing light conditions. Light that falls on any colored surface affects its appearance; it can make it brighter or more subdued. So before you select a color for a room, take into consideration the amount of light coming into that room, its direction, and its intensity. To do this, make a note of the windows in the room, recording their size and direction. For instance, windows with northern or eastern exposures introduce cool light into a room. Windows facing south or west get direct sunlight, generally for more hours of the day, and so fill the room with warmer light. Therefore, pale or cool colors will appear rather cold in northern or eastern light, while warm and bright colors will look very hot and intense in southern or western light.

THE THREE BASIC COLOR SCHEMES

There are many ways of combining colors, but the three most commonly used and most successful methods are known as monochromatic, related, and complementary. A *monochromatic* scheme is created by using a single color in various degrees of intensity. In essence, the gradations of this one color are continuously repeated throughout the room to create the overall effect. By repeating the different tones of one hue, a most restful mood is created. A monochromatic scheme makes a good backdrop for colorful accessories. If you select blue for your monochromatic scheme, the tones would range from deep blue to pale sky blue. To create a really successful monochromatic scheme, use these tones in all their gradations throughout the room—walls, draperies, upholstery fabrics, and floor covering.

A *related* color scheme is created from those hues adjacent to each other on the color wheel; their common denominator, another color, links them. For instance, you might pick green-blue, adding yellow; or yellow, adding orange and red. Alternatively, you could start with yellow and then add yellow-green or yellow-orange. In general, a related scheme is most refreshing; it gains in interest when the intensity of the colors are varied. The accent colors you select to enhance this scheme depend on the hues you choose for the overall scheme. However, black and white look good with all colors, because they always bring out the true quality of every color on the color wheel.

A *complementary* scheme is created by utilizing colors on opposite sides of the color wheel, such as red and blue or green and red. Because they are strongly contrasting, they introduce a lively and vibrant look. For this reason they need careful distribution in a room. It is wise to let one color predominate; the secondary color should be used for smaller areas. When a vivid color and its complement need to be toned down, you can reduce their values by adding gray. When you combine a pair of opposite colors in a room, you introduce both coolness and warmth, which make an interesting combination and an attractive background for furnishings.

Unusual Color Combinations

Interior designers are most adept at combining colors for unique effects. Here are some of their suggestions.

Jane Victor, A.S.I.D. [American Society of Interior Designers], has utilized some unique color schemes to create an individual look in a standard living room. For instance, she will take a strong, vibrant color, splash it throughout an entire room, and then highlight it with paler accent colors. Some of her combinations include: purple accented by pink and cooled by white; wine balanced with silver gray and spiced with pale blue; midnight blue flashed with red and toned down by white.

Joan Blutter, F.A.S.I.D. [Fellow of American Society of Interior Designers], believes that an unusual color scheme not only stamps a room with great personality but also says much about the occupants. When talking to clients for whom she is creating an environment, she always tries to elicit their favorite colors and then works from there. Some of her striking color combinations are chocolate brown enlivened with pink, sky blue, or other pastel tones; deep coral spiced with apple green or moss green and highlighted with white; autumnal colors such as brown, gold, and orange mingled together and softened by sand tones. Joan points out that when using either a vibrant color or one that is dark it's a good idea to add white accents both to highlight the basic color and to cool it down.

Use a Style of Furniture for Individuality

It is possible to introduce a highly personalized environment in a room through the use of a particular style or period of furniture. Your choice of furniture not only expresses your personal taste and puts your own stamp on a room but also creates the mood and the overall look.

There are numerous styles to choose from. The one you select depends on your personal preferences and, naturally, the look you want to produce. If you are a traditionalist, then obviously your tastes will lean toward English and French designs from the eighteenth century, or perhaps American Colonial, Early American, or Federal. Although genuine antiques are available today, they are often prohibitive in price. However, many leading furniture manufacturers produce authentic reproductions that are well made and exact down to the last detail. The most popular styles are Early American, English Georgian, and French Provincial. When any one of these styles is used throughout a room, it produces a harmonious and cohesive look that makes a definitive statement. When using a period style, always select accessories from the same period or ones that blend in well with the furniture and are traditional in feeling. Good reproductions are generally available. Do not mingle modern accessories with traditional furnishings if you are trying to produce a totally pure traditional style.

When furnishing with period pieces, be sure the rest of the room is in keeping with them. For example, select a window treatment that has a traditional feeling to it and a floor covering that blends in. Upholstery fabrics and wall coverings should also reflect the period and style of the furniture.

Many people favor oriental designs. Again, it is possible to buy both the genuine thing as well as reproductions to create a Far Eastern ambience. The rules mentioned above also apply when creating this kind of room. Stay with accessories and other furnishings that reflect the oriental look, whether it be Chinese or Japanese, to create harmony and purity of design throughout.

If you prefer a contemporary look, then modern designs should be used to create this sleek, sophisticated environment. Today there is a wide selection of designs to choose from by noted American and foreign designers and manufacturers. Once again, I repeat that the same rules must be followed: Select accessories and furnishings that reflect the modern pieces and preserve the contemporary mood.

A Breakdown of Styles

EIGHTEENTH-CENTURY ENGLISH

The most popular furniture from this period is commonly known as Georgian. It was made during the reigns of George I, George II, and George III, who ruled England in the eighteenth and early nineteenth centuries. This period is collectively known as the "golden age of design." Such gifted craftsmen as Thomas Chippendale, George Hepplewhite, the two Adam brothers, and Thomas Sheraton created exquisite furniture designs. All of the styles they created are still favorites today—and with good reason. The pieces have great elegance of design, are classic in feeling, and still work beautifully in twentieth-century homes. Woods used in reproductions are generally mahogany or walnut, with brocade, silk, satin, or velvet upholstery on chairs and sofas. The breakfront secretary-bookcase with glass doors, the Pembroke table, the tilt-top tea table, the circular rent table, the hunt table, the Chinese Chippendale chair, and sofas with camelbacks and serpentine fronts are a few of the representative pieces that are still widely used today.

If it's a formal, elegant feeling you wish to produce, then this style is certainly ideal.

FRENCH PROVINCIAL

Regional copies of court furniture made during the reigns of Louis XIII, Louis XIV, Louis XV, and Louis XVI are known as French Provincial. One of the most popular styles still used today, it is divided into two categories. Country Provincial was created by local craftsmen from available woods—mainly oak, chestnut, beech, and elm. Although copied from court styles, Country Provincial dispensed with gilt, painted decoration, and marquetry. Wood was unfinished or rubbed down, usually with wax. Most chairs had rush seats. City Provincial, also simpler than the court styles, was a little more sophisticated than Country Provincial furniture. Lacking elaborate decoration, it nevertheless had more upholstery; sofas and chairs had upholstered backs, seats, arm pads, and arms. Tables and chests were more refined as well, although they retained a rustic character. French Provincial reproductions have woods that are either waxed to bring out their natural graining or painted in antique colors or white. Upholstery fabrics used are generally cotton, tweed, wool, cotton velvet, and leather or suede—or man-made materials that simulate the latter two.

French Provincial is ideal for creating a country look in a room, one that has a degree of elegance and charm without being too stylized and formal.

EARLY AMERICAN

This furniture style springs from the early American craftsmen. It is rustic in character, having stemmed from the various peasant styles of Europe. The most well-known design of this period (1650–1700) is Pennsylvania German furniture, commonly called Pennsylvania Dutch. The woods most commonly used in reproductions are maple, oak, ash, pine, and hickory. Representative pieces are the Windsor chair and love seat, rocking chair, butterfly table, Shaker chest, ladder-back chair, and the rush-seated Carver armchair. Fabrics used for upholstered pieces are generally simple, such as cotton, linen, cotton velvet, wool, and chintz.

Early American introduces a mellow country ambience in a room, one that is slightly more rustic in feeling.

MODERN

This term is applied to various styles of furniture that have developed since the early twenties. The styles are an outgrowth of modern architecture. They first appeared in Germany and Scandinavia, later spreading to Italy, England, and the United States. The great modern designs have come from Ludwig Mies van der Rohe, Le Corbusier, Marcel Breuer, and Eero Saarinen, all of whom were architects; and from furniture designers Charles Eames, Jens Risom, T. H. Robsjohn-Gibbings, George Nelson, and Edward J. Wormley, many of whose designs have become classics.

The design characteristics of modern furniture include a purity of line, form, and materials. Many pieces have a light, floating look. Great use is made of wood, steel, chrome, glass, marble, slate, and plastic. Shapes are generally classically simple and clean-cut; some are molded or fitted to match the contours of the body.

Modern furniture creates a sleek, sophisticated ambience that works particularly well in a room of modern architectural design. Although the look is sparse and understated, it has a great sense of elegance that springs from its simplicity. Warmth can be introduced through the use of modern accessories, art, sculpture, and plants.

Flexible Furniture Arrangements

In the past few years many interior designers have been advocating more flexible furniture arrangements, casual groupings that can be changed easily to suit different living needs. It is possible to create these seating arrangements through the use of the latest sectional sofas and chairs, along with ottomans and modular seating of different heights. The basic idea behind the newest flexible groupings is their mobility—as opposed to the stylized arrangements of the past, where sofas and chairs remained stationary at all times and could not be moved for fear of ruining the look of a room.

Interior designers have had great success with these flexible arrangements, since they enable the occupants of a room to introduce a new look quite easily—without spoiling the overall appearance of the room. In a flexible arrangement pieces generally flow into each other, with seating balanced by small occasional tables that can also be moved at will. This new way of arranging furniture is particularly suited to our more casual life-styles because it is not structured in any way.

A flexible furniture arrangement can also be created with standard pieces of furniture and does not necessarily have to be composed of sectionals. The key is to create several loose, airy groupings within the room that adjoin but do not intrude on each other, groupings that can be intermingled, when required, for parties and entertaining.

Other Elements that Introduce a Unique Look

A variety of other elements help to bring a look of individuality and personality to a room of standard design and shape.

WALLS

You can create interesting effects in a living room by treating the walls with imagination. Apart from painting them a striking color, you can give them a whole new look through the use of a number of other materials. They can be lined with wood paneling or upholstered with fabric, leather, suede, or man-made materials that simulate these materials. Interesting wall coverings abound today, such as charmingly patterned wallpaper, vinyl, and grass cloth, all of which introduce unique effects. Scenic and mural wallpaper produce eye-catching overtones that are often three-dimensional in feeling; alternatively, you can apply mirror tiles to one wall to produce illusionistic qualities and expand the space. Hand-painted murals also bring an exciting look to walls and lift them out of the ordinary.

Whichever treatment you select, be sure it blends well with your overall decorating scheme, the furniture style you are using, and all the other furnishings within the room.

FLOORS

The floor of a living room can be treated in such a way that it introduces a new look and underscores the individuality created by other furnishings. Today's modern area rugs are extremely well designed, have colorful and original patterns and textures, and are moderately priced. They help to define seating arrangements and specific areas within a room. At the same time, they add life, movement, and decorative interest underfoot. Oriental carpets and antique area rugs can be used to the same end; which you select will depend on the style and period of the furniture in the room.

Painted floors are very popular today, for they, too, make a decorative statement that adds extra individuality to the decor of a room. Interior designers recommend stripping the floor down to its natural color and then painting it several times in the shade of your choice. To withstand scuffs and abuse, the floor should be treated with several coats of polyurethane, which seals and protects. Stenciled floors, so common in Early American rooms, are making a comeback; many interior designers are now using them in place of carpets, wall-to-wall carpeting, and other floor products. Designs are stenciled onto a painted floor to simulate area rugs, tiles, and bricks.

Vinyl tiles can be put down in ingenious ways to simulate rugs and carpets. The designs are created by using two differently colored vinyl tiles in interesting patterns in the manner of soft floor coverings. Still other vinyl tiles simulate brick, marble, ceramic, and wood; they, too, can be used to produce unique effects.

WINDOWS

Standard windows might seem to defy good decoration, but this is not really the case. Numerous treatments work well with the average window; interesting new looks can be produced when imagination and skill are utilized. Like the walls and the floor, the treatment you use with windows should reflect the overall decor and be in step with the mood you are attempting to create.

A room with traditional overtones should be given a window treatment that underscores this, whether you use draperies and a valance, draperies in combination with a window shade, or cafe curtains. Shutters work well in a room that has a rustic country ambience, as do cafe curtains or stenciled window shades. The latter can also be laminated with a fabric that appears elsewhere in the room for an interesting coordinated effect. Vertical blinds, the latest narrow-slatted blinds, and simple floor-to-ceiling draperies are ideal in a room of contemporary design.

Other window treatments include such things as shoji screens, matchstick blinds, hand-painted sliding screens, fabric hung from panel tracks mounted on the ceiling. Whichever individualized treatment you select, remember that it should never be overwhelming or out of step with the rest of the decor.

Accessories Add a Personal Touch

Without accessories even a highly individualized room can look unfinished and a little cold. Accessories not only add that necessary finishing touch but say a lot about you, your tastes, and your preferences. They also help to imbue a room with personality and give it warmth, color, and textural play.

There are no basic rules about the type of accessories you should include in a living room. Your selection will depend on what you have already collected, your taste, the style of the room, its overall decor, and the space available. Obviously, a small living room requires less accessories than a large one, since too many items will give it a cluttered look. Conversely, a large room requires more accessories if it is not to look half finished.

When selecting your accessories, pay attention to their size in relation to the dimensions of the room. Small items will look lost in a large room; huge pieces will overwhelm a room that is small and confined. Accessories need to be carefully selected and arranged. Every object should be displayed with lots of flair and imagination, so that its total decorative value can be seen. When buying new accessories, always choose objects you know you can live with for a long time. Objects can often become banal and boring when they are not selected with care and thought.

Many objects fall into the category of accessories: lamps, paintings, prints, sculpture, ornaments, candles, wall plaques, decorative cushions, mirrors, clocks, native handicrafts, artifacts, and plants, to name just a few. All of them help to add character and a new dimension to a standard living room by reinforcing the individualized look you have created.

OVERLEAF This small living room was given great originality and unique looks through the ingenious decorating ideas of *Shirley Regendahl.* The secret of the room's success is, of course, the seating pit. The designer created this by building a platform at one end of the room. She carried the platform around under the windows to form a semicircle for the modular seating units. The units consist of four pieces—corner, armless, wedge, and ottoman—which provide complete versatility in room planning. Two corner units are used to form a small sofa opposite the pit for additional seating space. Units are upholstered in brown velvet, providing a dramatic contrast with the white vinyl tiles with marble finish that cover the plywood platform and shelf under the windows. Since the room was relatively small, accessories were kept to a minimum, except for a variety of plants and a handsome collection of blue-and-white china on étagères that bring soft color accents into the room. Silvery blinds at the windows make a shimmering backdrop for the plants, some of which are potted while others are suspended from the ceiling. The platform becomes a spot for dining, where a chrome-and-glass table and cane-and-chrome chairs provide comfort in a small space. According to the designer, it is easy for a carpenter to copy this platform.

Interior designer *Joan Blutter,* F.A.S.I.D. [Fellow of the American Society of Interior Designers], gave a highly individualized look to her Chicago living room through a little brilliant designing. The key to the overall scheme is the arrangement of the furniture. Instead of aligning seating pieces against the wall or in a standard grouping, she positioned them in the middle of the floor. The brown sofa and chairs are centered around a unique blue and white area rug and a giant-sized white-lacquered coffee table. Completing the grouping on the other side of the rug is a black leather chair (not visible), African drum table, and plants. Oriental rugs are placed on the perimeter of the room and lead out to the hall. They are set off beautifully against the unusual wood floor, as is the rug in the center of the room. Modern art makes its own definitive statement on the walls, introducing color and pattern in a room with unique features. Track lighting and spot lights hidden among the varied plants provide illumination. The designer points out that the furniture arrangement is extremely flexible for everyday living and entertaining, since chairs and sofa can be swung around or moved easily to accommodate large groups. She recommends this type of unusual grouping to give a whole new look to the standard apartment living room.

americana
americana

One way to introduce a focal point in a living room is to use freestanding case pieces brought together to form an interesting center for artifacts and the like. These pieces comprise a unit that is full of visual interest as a display area for books, accessories, and plants. It is also highly practical since it contains storage cupboards, a bar, and drawers for smaller items. Balanced on either side by plants, the unit covers most of the main wall and serves as the anchor for the furniture in the rest of the room. A long sofa, serviced by chrome-and-glass coffee tables, faces the unit and is backed up by a library table. The fluffy white rug is a luxurious touch. The beauty of this type of focal point is that it can be moved easily to a new home should you decide to relocate, as opposed to a mock fireplace or other tacked-on architectural elements.

OVERLEAF Designer *Remy Chatain* came up with a surprising but rather apt combination of the old and the new to create a special mood in a city apartment. Cleverly teamed together are such things as a wall covering in old caftan colors, shade cloth vertical blinds in white, English antiques, and some modern pieces. The verticals move across the windows where the warm background of the traditional wallpaper pattern leaves off, crisply solving the problems involved in windows plus terrace door. In so doing, they add considerably to the overall charm inherent in the standard living room. On the terrace side (shown), the verticals were hung forward, in front of an overhanging beam, to give a camouflaging floor-to-ceiling effect full play. Then, for the sake of unity, the verticals were repeated at the other windows in the room. Within this mellow setting of contemporary and eighteenth-century styles, a brown suede sofa is companion to an armchair and ottoman upholstered in fabric matching the wall covering. Queen Anne chairs are also upholstered with this fabric to create a sense of unity throughout. An antique pine secretary next to the window echoes the room-heightening points made so effectively by the verticals and the striped wall covering. The eighteenth-century English drop-leaf table, occasional tables from the same era, and other antique pieces are balanced by a white-lacquered end table holding shells and, on the other side of the room, small cubes where an orchid collection is displayed. Here *Remy Chatain* illustrates how an eclectic mingling of modern and period furniture and accessories come together to produce a wholly different look in a squared-off living room in a typical high-rise building.

A large barnlike living room was given enormous character through some clever decorating by interior designer *Everett Brown,* F.A.S.I.D. To give the room a look of individuality and lift it out of the ordinary, he used wood paneling partway up the walls. He then filled in the gap between the paneling and the ceiling with a small-scale red and black check fabric. A floral-patterned border was run around the room at ceiling level to add a finishing touch. The paneling at once introduced warmth and set the traditional mood of the room. The designer then furnished it with such things as a period desk, end tables, and elegant upholstered pieces. To fulfill the mood of the room, the windows were given a traditional treatment. Tieback draperies made of a red-and-white toile were topped by matching valances, and both windows were finished with shades laminated with the red and black check fabric. The only contemporary touch in the room is the red and black checked wall-to-wall carpet, but it blends in beautifully, underscoring the basic red and black color scheme highlighted by white and mellowed by the wood tones of the paneling. The furniture grouping is loose and airy, but the French reproduction chair and the Queen Anne wing chair can be moved up to the sofa when a more intimate grouping is required.

OVERLEAF To introduce a focal point and give interesting dimensions to an otherwise dull room of standard design, interior designer *Shirley Regendahl* used several unique architectural elements. She added a false ceiling in a squared-off design, mirrored one wall, and then added bookshelves. The bookshelf unit becomes the center of interest, a visually exciting space filled with books, shells, and other accessories. It also reflects light and bounces it back into the room. The unit immediately dictated the arrangement of the furniture. The designer created an interesting arrangement with three upholstered sofas, which are close enough for easy conversation while still maintaining an open look. The sides of the sofas consist of brown maplewood with an unusual woven insert, a warm contrast against the beige textured fabric. An area rug in soft tones of brown, blue, and beige anchors two chrome cubes, while two white-lacquered cubes hold lamps and plants. The designer has stated that the wall unit is simple and not very expensive to build. Mirror tiles can be used in the individual spaces. The shelves are made of plywood, which is then painted white.

THAT MAN CARTWRIGHT
The Searchers
Edsel
KID YOU NOT
JACK PAAR
The Seance
ONCE AN EAGLE

In this small modern living room a combination of furniture and accessories introduced a much-needed visual center of interest. The main wall was painted a soft yellow and then a long console table was placed against it. This was partnered with three contemporary benches. Once these items were positioned, a modern painting was hung on the wall above them to create a striking diamondlike effect. It is balanced by a handsome lamp and flowers. This focal point acted as a guide for the arrangement of the rest of the furniture, including two sofas, a coffee table, and an easy chair. Groupings such as this are the simplest way to introduce visual interest in a room without a focal point.

OVERLEAF This exciting modern living room is located in an old-fashioned Manhattan apartment. It has been made highly individualistic through skillful decorating and a clever choice of furnishings. Interior designer *Leif Pedersen,* A.S.I.D., transformed a dull, standard room by using such elements as upholstered walls, modular seating, good lighting, and lots of plants. To hide marred and cracked walls, he padded and "quilted" them in a soft coffee-colored fabric and then bleached the floor to a pale natural tone, coating it with polyurethane for durability. Two old-fashioned windows situated next to each other were hidden with white narrow-slatted blinds; the wall between them was lined with a floor-to-ceiling mirror to create a sense of depth and dimension and to balance the white blinds. Sectional seating of different heights was arranged in a U-shape and centered around an area rug in soft pinks and greens. The brown and beige upholstery fabric has the look of needlepoint. The seating is serviced by a chrome-and-glass coffee table. Three bleached wood cubes, lined up at one end of the room, display a plant, a piece of sculpture, and other accessories; they help to enclose the seating area and create an intimate feeling. Floor lamps and track lighting (not visible) provide soft illumination throughout. Splashes of intense color are introduced through the use of modern paintings. To give the room a new look, the flexible furniture arrangement can be regrouped, as can the cubes and plants. This designer proves the point that a modern ambience can be superimposed on old-style architecture quite successfully.

Interior designer *Ron Budney,* A.S.I.D. [American Society of Interior Designers], used a variety of elements to add a new dimension to a typical apartment living room. These included color, unusual window treatments, and the latest sectional furniture. It is color that sets the mood and lifts the apartment out of the ordinary—a play of vivid green highlighted by intense splashes of white. The carpet color matches the green walls, while white shows up on the ceiling, at the windows, in the trim on the bookcase, furniture, and accessories. To camouflage standard windows the designer hung white, sheer curtains close to the glass and then added trellis panels painted white. The effect is trim and tailored and, of course, eliminates the need for dust-catching draperies. The trellis panels can simply be lifted off wall hooks when the sheer curtains have to be laundered. The sectional seating, composed of two sofas and ottomans, can be arranged in many ways. Here the designer used an L-shape made up of the sofas and one ottoman, placing the second ottoman closer to the coffee table. The unusual golden burl coffee table adds color, texture, and balance to the seating area. To make the bookcase more interesting, the designer added molding painted white. He placed two white palm tree lamps on a library table behind the sofa. An oriental statue on a pedestal fills up a corner. The finished room has a highly individualistic look thanks to clever decorating.

Shiny silver, stark white, and shocking pink are the colors of this sophisticated apartment, designed for a New York career couple by *Virginia Frankel,* A.S.I.D. Apart from wanting a sleek, modern ambience, the couple also asked the designer to eliminate the sterile look of the living room, which had no architectural interest whatsoever. The decorating ideas it illustrates are applicable anywhere. For example, note the use of vertical blinds to serve a dual role. Acting as a glamorous window treatment that flashes silver along an entire wall, the blinds at the same time conceal the "works" of the wall—steps and a door leading to a terrace at one end, a radiator and air conditioner underneath the main windows. The blinds can easily be drawn aside to permit access to the terrace; at night they can be tilted silghtly to let the lights of the city twinkle in. They also make a stunning reflective backdrop for the lush grouping of greenery, both potted and tubbed, which creates a lovely indoor garden. Starting in the foyer (not shown), bands of silver Mylar turn the corner into the living room and form a super-graphic against the white wall at left, linking various areas of the apartment to one another. Artifacts are interestingly spaced and beautifully lit by spotlights mounted on a ledge built for this purpose behind the modular sofa at left. Designer Frankel cites this as an obvious and practical alternative to ceiling spots, which would have been more expensive. Glass and chrome tables have an open, airy look, reflecting light and appearing to float. The bare floor with its dark stain anchors the nubby white sofas and the pink and white area rug. Several ottomans (only one of which is visible) covered in fabric that matches the pillows can be moved around for flexible seating.

"Like floating in space" is the way the owners of this apartment in a remodeled tenement describe life in their white and beige living room. Because the room is less than twelve feet wide, the space was expanded visually with white walls, white built-in furniture, and a white carpet. If a white carpet in a city apartment seems impractical, it's not, since this carpet is made of soil-resistant nylon in a luxurious, dense plush. The room, typical of many standard remodeling jobs, could have looked quite ordinary without the flowing built-in furniture and white-lacquered end tables and coffee table. Paintings, pillows, and accessories also add drama and an original look. The Peruvian wall hanging is balanced by a modern painting on the opposite wall, while books, red lacquer accents, and a variety of pillows add a splash of color to the all-white shell. Simple window shades underscore the sleek simplicity of the room. Incidentally, behind the sophisticated look of this room lies a very modest budget; the owner, an architect, designed and built all the furniture himself.

It is possible to create an individualized look in a living room through the use of a particular period of furniture or one of unique style. Here a small, ordinary living room gains oriental overtones through the use of pieces of Far Eastern design that are contemporary in feeling for twentieth-century life-styles. Two rattan sofas in a sable brown finish are upholstered in a fabric with a traditional oriental cherry blossom pattern. End tables and accent pieces also have a Far Eastern feeling. This is underscored by the simply decorated shell, which is somewhat Japanese in mood. Standard windows were treated to split bamboo blinds and the plain wood floor was left bare except for a woven wool rug. The look is one of easy elegance, with the emphasis on understatement in the oriental manner.

OVERLEAF A sense of the Victorian era comes alive in this living room in an apartment located in a modern high-rise building. Its unique look was created through the use of antique furniture and accessories, traditional fabrics, and old-fashioned treatments at two standard windows. The full, flowing draperies were topped with frilled valances, each edged with a blue and white spotted fabric. The same fabric is repeated on the hems of the draperies. A coordinated floral fabric was used on the sofa and two chairs to create a feeling of harmony plus color balance in the blue and gold room. Such things as the antique oriental area rug, lacquered tray table in front of the sofa, and antique occasional tables add to the overall period ambience. Decidedly Victorian in feeling are the carved wooden brackets holding blue and white china as well as the lacquered box on a tall stand placed underneath for balance.

This long living room had no distinctive features, but it was given an interesting look through the use of freestanding case pieces grouped around three walls. The pieces provide space for displaying all manner of items, including books and accessories, as well as storage cupboards in the bases. An unusual painting situated on the end wall creates a three-dimensional effect and turns the wall into the focal point. The case pieces form the perfect backdrop for the long sofas, composed of sectional pieces, and also introduce architectural overtones in a bland-looking room. Ottomans under the counter can be pulled out to become part of the conversation area when required. This room proves the point that a clever choice of furniture and a good arrangement can introduce a highly individualized look.

BK
Home Decorating

In this spacious living room, designed by *Robert Metzger,* where white creates a cool shell, overstuffed armless chairs and ottomans are grouped in several spacious arrangements. They produce two distinct and separate seating/conversation areas yet are part of each other because there are no visual blocks. The red and white patterned sectionals, placed at angles, make up the bulk of the room's furnishings. The repeated use of square and rectangular forms creates a feeling of balance and harmony and keeps the room looking delicate and uncluttered. This bold-patterned grouping is accented by bright, solid-colored throw pillows in pink, red, and purple. Small lacquer and rattan coffee tables divide the seating effectively. The bright colors are balanced by the abundant use of white on the floor, ceiling, sling chairs, and canvas window shades. Unusual pieces of sculpture, a dramatic painting, and lots of plants add finishing touches.

Double the Function and Comfort of Bedrooms

The decorative look for bedrooms has changed radically in the past few years. Leading interior designers have utilized a fresh approach to create a sitting room ambience rather than a total bedroom mood.

This whole new feeling is achieved mainly through the elimination of chests, armoires, wardrobes, and the old-fashioned bedroom suite, all of which helped to produce a "storage room" look that was cumbersome and unappealing. It is also achieved by the inclusion of other furnishings that give the room additional comfort, convenience, and a lovely appearance that is aesthetically pleasing.

Nowhere is this updated look more appropriate than in an apartment or town house bedroom, where space is often at a premium. It gives a bedroom a new dimension for round-the-clock living, turns it into a spot for relaxation, and helps it to function as a second sitting room.

A variety of elements are necessary to create this environment. Good design is naturally of prime importance, since a proper and well-balanced plan means correct utilization of space and use of all furnishings to their best advantage. But aside from this, furniture, soft furnishings, wall and floor coverings, lighting, and accessories should also be chosen with great care to produce the correct ambience. Most importantly, the color scheme must not be overlooked, since this helps to introduce a particular mood and sets the backdrop for all of the furnishings. Of course, it is not always possible to double *both* the function and comfort of bedrooms. Often only one of these requirements can be dealt with in an overall scheme because of space and/or budget limitations. But with a little imagination and ingenuity you can certainly give your bedroom new mannerisms and make it live up to its potential as a room to be *lived in* and enjoyed.

Before you start tackling your bedroom scheme, make a floor plan following the rules outlined in the first chapter. Also buy a template of furniture shapes to create arrangements of furniture; don't forget that it's so much easier to push furniture around on paper than it is to do so physically. The paper plan also acts as a buying guide and prevents costly mistakes. Once you have measured the room, made your floor plan, and created furniture arrangements, you can set about decorating the bedroom. Here are some basic guidelines to help you do this successfully and achieve the best results.

Color Schemes for Bedrooms

Color is important in any room of an apartment, but it is especially so in a bedroom, where restfulness and a sense of tranquility are essential.

Consider your favorite colors and then eliminate those that you feel are too bright or too strong. They may work well in a living room or other general living quarters, but they can often be disturbing in a bedroom, where a sense of repose is vital. Instead, select gentler colors that you know you can live with at all times, especially ones that produce a peaceful effect in the evening when you are tired.

Interior designer *Leif Pedersen,* A.S.I.D., favors monochromatic color schemes for bedrooms since these are particularly restful. The eye is not jarred by sharply contrasting colors and, of course, a monochromatic scheme helps to expand the feeling of space through optical illusion. Although this designer agrees that pale pink is too girlish for a master bedroom shared by a man and a woman, he does favor certain deeper pinks, such as dark rose and that unusual color called "ashes of roses," which is a pink slightly tinged with gray. He also likes a deep coral scheme as well. According to this designer, these three shades add a degree of warmth and lend themselves to a variety of accent colors, such as white, moss green, and brown.

Apple green balanced by deep fir green and accented with white is another scheme he recommends for its fresh appeal and restfulness. On the other side of the color spectrum, he suggests dark gray fabric-covered walls—the color of flannel, to be exact—and matching wall-to-wall carpeting, enlivened by sharp blue, silver gray, and a light dash of burgundy in smaller accents. The designer explains that this all-gray shell lends itself beautifully to modern furnishings, such as pieces made of chrome and glass, or steel and glass, as well as interesting art and accessories.

Jane Victor, A.S.I.D., another leading New York designer, recently designed an eye-catching bedroom for clients that was visually exciting yet also peaceful. The predominant color was a midnight blue, which she used on the walls and the ceiling. The same color was selected for tieback draperies at the windows and for some of the upholstery fabrics. A modern four-poster with a canopy, made entirely of wood, was lacquered white and given a white fur throw. The white relieved the preponderance of midnight blue, as did a wall of closets lined with mirrors. A vibrant contrasting color was used underfoot in the wall-to-wall carpeting patterned in midnight blue, red, and white, but the overall effect in the room was one of tranquil blueness. Good lighting and interesting accessories completed the room, which served as a second sitting room thanks to the inclusion of a desk, sofa, and chairs upholstered in white.

A charming bedroom just completed by Chicago interior designer *Joan Blutter,* F.A.S.I.D., features yellow throughout. This designer thinks yellow is a marvelous "unisex" color, one that a man feels equally at home around. It is also sunny, cheerful, and tranquil. Joan used a small-scale floral fabric with a yellow background throughout the room. It was shirred onto the walls, hung at the windows, and used on the bed in the form of a comforter, dust ruffle, pillow shams, and quilted headboard. The wall-to-wall carpeting was of the same yellow, selected to create a feeling of coordination and harmony. No other contrasting colors were introduced into this all-yellow shell, except for white bedside tables. The dressing table was of chrome and glass, as was a coffee table placed between two love seats upholstered in the same floral print.

When interior designer *Virginia Frankel,* A.S.I.D., came to decorate the master bedroom in her new apartment, she settled on white. This color was used throughout the entire room—on the walls, ceiling, floor, at the windows, and on the bed. However, she created a lot of visual interest by using diverse textures, such as linen on the walls and at the window, a wool wall-to-wall carpet on the floor, and a furry throw on the bed. This textural play dispensed with any feeling of coldness, as did hot pink and green throw pillows on the bed, a parrot green trim on the windows, and the mellow wood tones of various antiques. Apart from being fresh and luxurious to live in, the room is filled with a sense of peacefulness (see photo at end of chapter).

As pointed out earlier, certain colors do introduce a special mood.

A tranquil mood is created by the soft, restful colors, such as light blue, apple green, primrose or daffodil yellow, white peach or apricot, all the beige and sand tones, and pearl gray.

A cool mood springs from white, deeper greens, sharp blues, and a combination of black and white.

A sunny mood is produced through the use of bright yellow, shrimp, coral, tangerine, and bright gold.

A warm mood comes from the very hot and intense colors, such as red, terracotta, purple, vivid orange, and all the rich autumnal shades.

Naturally, you can select any of these colors for a bedroom scheme, depending on the kind of mood you want to create. But remember that some of the more intense tones can become boring and overpowering after a time, so study colors carefully before making your final choice. Don't forget that you have to live with a color scheme for a long time and it is costly to keep redecorating.

Make a Bedroom Function for More General Living

CHOICE OF FURNITURE

You can double the function and comfort of bedrooms by choosing your furniture selectively. Apart from the bed(s), you can go in almost any direction you want when it comes to the other pieces. What you select depends on your taste, your living needs, and the size of the room.

A writing desk and chair are popular additions to today's bedrooms. They introduce a sitting room atmosphere and provide a spot for letter writing and paperwork. Choose a desk and chair that echoes the mood and style created by your other furnishings. For example, if the bedroom is contemporary, pick out a modern desk, a chrome-and-glass or Parsons table, and a chair that is of similar modern style. A traditional room requires a desk and chair of period design. Lightly scaled pieces are readily available today in both modern and period designs; they are made especially for apartment rooms that are confined and of small dimensions.

Étagères can be used in a bedroom, where they make attractive display centers for interesting objects, books, and plants. They also help to give a bedroom new mannerisms by adding highly decorative overtones and lots of visual interest, giving you a chance to show off treasured personal possessions. There are all kinds of étagères available in chrome and glass, steel and glass, plastic with simulated wood-grain finish, and a variety of wood tones as well. Designs are both modern and traditional to suit different furniture styles.

A love seat, small sofa, or chair plus ottoman in combination with a small occasional table for a lamp and magazines can be utilized to create a conversation area in the bedroom or a spot for relaxation, whether this be for sewing, reading, listening to music, or watching television. This type of small grouping does much to increase the comfort and function of any bedroom regardless of its size.

OTHER ELEMENTS

You can introduce further comfort into the average apartment bedroom if you pay attention to certain other elements and select them carefully.

The *floor covering* is naturally very important in this room. It should provide necessary comfort, warmth, and a luxurious feeling, as well as good looks.

Wall-to-wall carpeting is a popular choice. Many types and designs available today blend with both contemporary and traditional decor. Colors are particularly exciting, with a wide range to choose from to fulfill your overall color scheme. Apart from the qualities just mentioned, wall-to-wall carpeting also helps to soundproof a bedroom and increases the feeling of space underfoot through visual illusion.

Area rugs work well in a bedroom. You can use a large rug that stretches almost from wall to wall or select several smaller ones for the foot of the bed and on either side. You might consider orientals, antique area rugs, or rugs of modern design, which are highly decorative and well made. The flokati rug is a favorite with many people because of its long-haired, fluffy texture, as are imitation fur rugs made of synthetic fibers. These have a similar luxurious appearance and feel soft to the touch. Vinyl or wood floors can be rather cold in a bedroom. They should always be enhanced with area rugs. But whichever type of rug you select, be sure it underscores the decorative theme prevalent in the room.

The *wall covering* you select for your bedroom largely depends on your personal tastes, the size of the room and, of course, the amount of money you have to spend. You can either paint the walls in a color of your choice or you can cover them with various materials. Fabrics stapled to the walls do much to introduce decorative overtones. They add a feeling of warmth and help soundproof, too.

Depending on your basic theme, you can pick a patterned fabric or a solid color. The fabric can be hung flat against the wall or shirred. Designer *Leif Pedersen* likes to create an upholstered look on walls, which he says adds a rich, luxurious feeling in a bedroom. He does this by nailing vertical strips of wood, running from floor to ceiling, along the walls. Cotton wadding is then attached to the strips of wood and across the entire length of the walls. The fabric is stretched over the cotton wadding and stapled into position. The result is a padded look that is most effective. Fabrics suitable for use on bedroom walls include cotton, linen, chintz, wool, velvet, cotton velvet, and silk.

Many other interior designers advocate the use of sheets on the walls of a bedroom. A lovely custom-designed effect can be achieved when sheets are stapled to the walls and then repeated on the bed, at the windows for draperies, and even for upholstery on a chair or love seat. Sheets are popular for this decorating technique because they are well designed, easy to launder, and not all that expensive.

Attractive wallpaper and vinyl wall coverings can also be utilized to enhance a bedroom. A wide selection is currently available at reasonable prices.

Good *lighting* is vital in a bedroom because it does much to introduce a particular mood and a sense of comfort. It should be well planned, with the fixtures carefully distributed to create the right effect. Avoid harsh or overly strong lighting in a bedroom, as this soon becomes tiring. Instead, use table and floor lamps that are correctly shaded to introduce a soft, subdued effect, one that is pleasing aesthetically and easy to live with. In addition to bedside lamps, which are a must, other lighting fixtures should be included in different parts of the room for proper illumination throughout. Select lighting fixtures that are in keeping with the basic decorating theme and enhance the appearance of the room.

A *TV set* is a standard addition in many bedrooms today. It certainly expands the function and comfort of this room, helping to give it sitting-room mannerisms. The type and size of the set you select depends on your needs, the dimensions of the room, available space, and the amount of money you wish to spend. A small set can be housed on a standard-type TV table, chest, or étagère if these are part of your furnishings. Or you can purchase a console that conceals the set when it is not in use. There are many designs available today in both traditional and modern styles. When placing a TV set in a bedroom, be sure that it is correctly positioned so that it can be viewed from the bed as well as from other points in the room where you might have created a conversation area.

One leading manufacturer is now producing a French Provincial armoire that contains a 25-inch TV set plus stereo equipment, including turntable, speakers, and storage space for records and tapes. This is an ideal piece to use when you want to create an entertainment center in the bedroom. It is possible to use a hi-fi in a bedroom provided that you have the available space for the turntable and speakers. When using individual components in various areas of the room, don't forget that the speakers should always be spaced eight feet apart for the best sound reproduction and listening comfort.

Furniture Arrangements

You can create fresh looks in a bedroom and add to its comfort by arranging furniture in new and different ways.

The bed does not necessarily have to be placed against the main wall in the traditional manner. Often you can create a different mood and make better use of space by positioning it elsewhere. It can go in front of a window, for example, where an unusual or interesting window treatment will create an eye-catching backdrop. By utilizing the window area, you free the main wall for another grouping of furniture, such as a desk, bookcases, étagères, or a pair of chairs and an occasional table.

A bed placed in the center of the room and fitted with a tailored spread, plus a mélange of throw pillows arranged on it, can become a spot for sitting and lounging during the day. Centralizing the bed in this way also frees wall space for other furniture.

You can divide a room by placing the bed a few feet away from the main wall and backing it up with a set of low chests that act as a headboard. The area created behind the bed can be transformed into a small dressing room, with the chests providing storage and display space. A long library or Parsons table can be used in the same manner; the free space can become a spot for letter writing and paperwork through the addition of a chair or stool.

If you want to include a writing desk in the bedroom and are short on space, use one next to the bed in place of a bedside table. This is a practical idea and frees wall space elsewhere in the room.

Bookshelves, whether built-in or freestanding, can be arranged on either side of the bed to create an interesting effect. The shelves at bed level act as end tables; while the other shelves can be well utilized for displaying books, accessories, and other personal possessions. If you are building the shelves on either side of the bed, it's often a good idea to carry them across the center of the wall above the bed. They then become an eye-catching headboard that is also practical and convenient. Chrome-and-glass étagères can also be used on either side of the bed in place of end tables.

Furniture that can be hung on the wall is also a marvelous asset in a bedroom. It brings new dimensions to the room, freeing floor space so that you can create a seating area within the room. All manner of wall-hung units are available today, including bookshelves with storage cupboards and drop-leaf work tops that double as desk or vanity, or both.

Personalize with Accessories

As was pointed out in the first chapter, accessories do much to add a finished look to a living room and also introduce highly personal overtones. They are equally important in a bedroom—or, for that matter, in any other room of an apartment.

Look at all of your favorite things, select those that would be most appropriate in a bedroom, and then go about arranging them in interesting ways. Here are some ideas from leading designers.

Chicago-based interior designer *Janet Shiff* likes to use collections of photographs in bedrooms she decorates for clients. Whenever possible Janet utilizes old-fashioned frames that she ferrets out in antique stores and thrift shops. She particularly favors Victorian and turn-of-the-century frames, which are often fanciful and elaborate; they are made of brass, silver, and wood. Janet suggests the use of a diverse collection of frames for the family photographs, which should be grouped together on a skirted or occasional table in a corner of the bedroom. She recommends the use of a lamp on the table to illuminate the photographs. If you cannot find any old-fashioned frames, select attractive ones made of silver, chrome, Plexiglas, or, alternatively, wood frames covered with fabric. You can also use a grouping of photographs on a wall if you prefer this idea.

Joyce Vagasy, an interior designer, architect, and fabric designer, collects jade. She displays this on wall-hung glass shelves in a corner of her bedroom. The items are arranged according to color and size. Joyce recommends using glass shelves for collections of decorative objects; they are light, airy-looking, and show the items off to best advantage by not competing with them.

New York interior designer *John Elmo* is a great book lover. He believes that books can be included in a bedroom to make a highly decorative and personal statement. He often uses two sets of floor-to-ceiling bookshelves at each end of a wall to create a kind of alcove effect, with a desk or love seat placed in between. He intersperses the books with decorative objects, small paintings, photographs, and plants. As he has pointed out, the dust jackets add flashes of bright color to any scheme, while the other objects introduce a change of pace visually.

Renowned English interior designer *John Siddeley,* who now divides his time between London and New York, recommends the use of small sets of wall-hung shelves for displaying objects in a bedroom. He explained that this idea saves tabletop surfaces for other items and also helps to avoid breakages. John prefers glass-and-brass shelves or ones made of dark wood; he hangs them in a strategic spot where objects can easily be viewed. He suggests using crystal objects and fancy glass perfume bottles on glass shelves for a lovely shimmering look; delicate china objects should be used on mahogany shelves to create a contrast of color and texture.

To sum up, paintings, sketches, graphics and prints, plants, small trees, pillows, unusual candles, and lamps can all be used to add decorative overtones to a bedroom and create a very personal look. But remember the rules for accessorizing mentioned in the first chapter to produce the most striking effects. Don't add too many diverse items, which will produce a cluttered, often messy look. Always be selective.

HARVEST
ONCE AN EAGLE
ANTIQUES
THAT MAN CARTWRIGHT
The Encyclopedia of Furniture

PRECEDING PAGES The use of furnishings primarily associated with a living room rather than a bedroom create a sitting room ambience in this ordinary apartment bedroom. Within one room three distinct areas have been established. The room serves as a sleeping center, a living room, and an at-home office. This triple-purpose room is much more than just a place to sleep.

The bed alcove, which is the result of the building's basic construction, is artfully masked by the vertically striped fabric that covers all four walls. It provides a space to tuck the bed into so that it does not protrude completely into the room when it is opened. During the day the bed folds up inside the reserved area and the wood-paneled folding doors can be closed. On the reverse side of the panels the same fabric has been used to cover the wood so that the wall looks as though nothing is hidden behind it. When the doors are open, the wood panels serve as a frame for the area, setting it off visually.

The furniture arrangements clearly define the areas. A cream-colored cotton sofa is used both for casual entertaining and for small, informal business meetings. The glass desk and low tables seem to float on chrome bases and take up no visual space. A geometric-patterned carpet completes the sitting room ambience and reiterates the subtle pattern of the sofa fabric.

Floor-to-ceiling wood cabinets line most of one wall and are used to store office materials, a small typewriter, a TV, and a stereo unit. The clean, sleek lines of the furnishings and the contemporary feeling conveyed in the fabric and carpeting reflect the organized personality of the tenants.

OPPOSITE Through the clever use of sheets, it's easy to create a sophisticated bedroom with minimal expense. Today there is a wide range of patterns to choose from that will establish a theme and mood in an ordinary, square-shaped apartment bedroom.

Designer *Shirley Regendahl* used an exquisite sheet pattern, based on an Egyptian motif, to create this serene yet interesting master bedroom. The platform bed and the four walls are enveloped in the print's hieroglyphics, which are printed in bittersweet on an ivory background. The border print of the sheets, which represents the friezes of the winged goddess Isis, encloses the base of the bed and surrounds the room itself. The border, in accents of enamel blue and bittersweet, is also used at ceiling-molding height and along the bottom of the window curtains.

A coordinated comforter of scalloped design evokes the spirit of ancient cloisonné in a mélange of blues and highlights the colors used in the border print. A handsome bamboo chair, storage cabinet with open bookshelves, low wicker chest, and corner basket preserve the flavor and character of the central motif.

Across the room additional do-it-yourself techniques transform the nondescript casement windows into a decorative element. The winged Isis border of the sheet fabric is glued to the room-darkening shades, linking them decoratively with the rest of the room. Uprights set between the windows at once divide and unite them. The struts, which match the long curtains and cafe curtains framing the window treatment, are covered with the same hieroglyphic pattern that encloses the room.

A delicate combination of flowing neutrals set off by vibrant blues form a lovely background for a very special bedroom retreat. Plants and Egyptian accessories on the low chest, bookcase, and headboard complete the total mood.

OVERLEAF In this large master bedroom the furnishings reflect a complete commitment to the Early American period and make a strong statement for nostalgia.

A showcase of prized possessions and "finds" resulting from years of attending country antique auctions are used to create the total effect. The basic color scheme and mood are established through the use of a patterned wallpaper that masks the uneven plaster walls—often an unfortunate aspect when renting a spacious apartment in an older building. The same fabric is used to line the open corner hutch, which displays a collection of family photographs in frames that repeat the blue and white colors of the wallpaper.

An antique patchwork quilt in the same colors introduces a geometric pattern that blends harmoniously with the floral motif. A smaller patchwork quilt is used as a unique cover for a skirted table that serves as a bedside table. Small pieces of quiltwork are used to make decorative throw pillows for the double bed. Another form of handwork is displayed in the cross-stitch pillow covers that encase the sleeping pillows during daytime hours.

Additional charm and warmth are provided by the working fireplace, which is faced with delft blue tiles and framed in the same wood as the corner hutch. The wood, which frames the fireplace, is also used as ceiling molding to mask the unevenness of the ceiling at the point where it meets the walls.

Through the use of a few ingenious decorating ideas, a standard apartment bedroom can take on a fresh, clean, and open look that provides more than just a place to sleep. Interior designer *Yvette Gervey,* A.S.I.D., proves the point in this unusual bedroom, located in a modern apartment, which is of a typical medium-sized standard shape.

The eye-catching appeal of this room is achieved through an emphasis on quality, good taste, and the use of materials that are not usually associated with bedroom decorating. The king-sized bed, by its very dimensions, is the dominant piece of furniture in the room. By placing the bed in front of the window wall, it becomes a focal point in the room. The window serves as a "frame" for the bed, helping to make it stand out —but not too obtrusively.

The bed is set on a raised platform that covers most of the floor and is the appropriate size for the bed. The platform and the remainder of the floor are covered with a carpet that is alternately striped in various neutral tones. The carpet pattern helps to enlarge the room through visual illusion and the platform seems to melt into the floor level gracefully.

Two side beams (only one is visible) and the narrow strips of wall surrounding the windows are covered with a neutral quilted fabric. The same quilted fabric is utilized for the dust ruffle, the tailored, fitted bed cover, and the ten pillows, which are graduated in size and add a finishing touch to the bed.

The quilted wall areas partially enclose the bed, act as a unique type of headboard, and at the same time create a feeling of harmony and warmth, together with a custom-designed look. In keeping with the tailored feeling, vertical blinds that filter light yet don't intrude into the available space are used to cover the windows.

The charming wall hanging, which depicts a herd of elephants, lends movement, color, and interest to the bedroom, where a minimal amount of space has been made to work to best advantage.

Flexibility and durability are two key words in decorating a bedroom that will receive a great deal of traffic and must play many roles. This simple and attractive bedroom is well designed to serve many needs.

It works well as a sophisticated bedroom for a teenage girl who wants to entertain friends in a "den" atmosphere rather than in a feminine, traditional bedroom. The decorative scheme lends itself equally well to the demands of a den/study that provides sleeping comfort for guests or visiting in-laws who appreciate a regular bed rather than a convertible sofa.

Although it is not possible to tell by looking at the furniture, all the pieces are made of knockdown plastic. The furniture can either be disassembled easily for moving or it can be rearranged. For example, the tall étagères can be turned into a series of low bookcases. The table at the foot of the bed, has the same dimensions as the étagère shelves and can be stacked on top of one in an apartment with higher ceilings.

The clean, simple lines of the furniture create a sitting room ambience and give the room a look that is appropriate for an area that is more than just a place to sleep.

In this three-room apartment in a modern high-rise building, the bedroom has been turned into a den/sitting room that functions twenty-four hours a day.

Through the use of tailored fabrics, an unusual wall treatment for a bedroom environment, and a fresh approach to the placement of the double bed, this standard bedroom takes on a totally new appearance. The furniture arrangement frees the limited wall space of an average-sized bedroom so that it can accommodate a comfortable love seat in addition to the bed. The floating platform bed is placed into the room rather than against a wall, thereby becoming part of the daytime seating area. It is covered in a cream throw trimmed with a dark brown border. The large wool pillow shams repeat the tailored look and also provide a place to store the bed pillows during the day.

Two tall brown-lacquer bookcases make use of the vertical wall space rather than taking up floor space. A dressing table/desk is created by putting a narrow Parsons table between the two units. The wood-paneled walls, painted the same cream as the wool throw, maintain the den atmosphere and also muffle sound from the TV and the stereo hidden in the bookcase units.

Sleek, sophisticated prints, a geometric-patterned mirror frame, and clean-line vertical blinds at the windows (not visible) complete the mood.

Outstanding looks, total comfort, and a multipurpose environment can all be created in a bedroom for a relatively small outlay of money. A bedroom needs much less furniture than a living room, so once the basics have been purchased it's easy to cut down on expenditures to a certain extent.

This comfortable hideaway is streamlined and modern without being sterile. It is washed throughout in a cool mélange of blue and white, lightly accented with green in the fabric, which establishes a restful mood and makes the room comfortable to occupy. It is also a dual-purpose area since it has a seating corner for snacks and relaxation.

All of the basic furniture in the room was made to order by a carpenter. The bed base, coffee table, lamp table, and L-shaped banquette are of sturdy wood covered in an attractive wall covering that also adorns the four walls. The wall covering is pretrimmed, prepasted, and strippable, so it's an easy do-it-yourself project. It's a washable acrylic and is sturdy enough to use on the furniture as well as the walls.

The bed mattress is covered in a tailored spread; pillow shams are of ribbed cotton-velvet. The same durable fabric reappears on the comfortable, loose seating pads and back cushions that line the corner banquette and on the floor pillows.

Since space was at a premium, interior designer *Abbey Darer* dispensed with bedside tables and used modern light fixtures attached to the walls. The end table next to the banquette holds the telephone, lamp, and mini TV.

Interesting wall graphics, a modern wall sculpture, and lots of plants add further decorative dimensions to the room. Costs were kept low through thoughtful buying, ingenious decorating, and the utilization of practical do-it-yourself ideas.

THE METROPOLITAN MUSEUM OF ART 1870-1970

PRECEDING PAGES The country look of this garden apartment blends simplicity and taste in a manner that is fresh and charming.

Designer *Abbey Darer* created a bedroom that must serve both as a daytime working space for sewing as well as a nighttime area for sleeping. The need for a bright, well-lighted area and a place to store work materials during the evening were two demands that had to be met. A combination of southern and eastern exposures afforded a cheery corner with ample light and established the window area as a work center. A double-sided bookcase that houses fabrics, patterns, and other supplies was given a circular wood top and finished with a cloth to hide its practical mannerisms. In this new guise it also serves as a work surface. A portable sewing machine tucked away behind the table can easily be lifted onto the table during the day and stored out of sight at night. When the table is cleared it also doubles as a spot for breakfast.

The patchwork comforter, ruffled pillow shams, curtains, and tablecloth were all made in the corner sewing center and are well displayed in this comfortable, dual-purpose room. White-painted planking used to cover up damaged plaster walls adds an airy country feeling to the room. A medley of gingham and calico patterns in the vinyl flooring echoes the overall theme of the room decor. A brass bedstead, farmhouse chairs, planters, and a china dog complete this country setting in a city apartment.

OPPOSITE This terraced bedroom, with a magnificent view of the city harbor, is romantic and charming, but it needed tight design control to make it flow well from indoors out and back again.

Designer *Everett Brown,* F.A.S.I.D., artfully created just such a double-paced ambience by using an effective window treatment as the catalyst. Chocolate brown walls, almost the same shade as the parquet floor, form a restful background that lets the view play the dominant role. A handsome lambrequin frames the sliding glass doors and the window shades.

The gold, yellow, and white pattern that appears on the lambrequin, ceiling, bedspread, dust ruffle, tieback curtains, and laminated window shades demonstrates the effectiveness of using one pattern throughout. It creates a coordinated, custom-designed look. The paler colors balance the darker walls beautifully, as does the white area rug. Bright yellow is picked up in the lining for the canopied bed, the wood molding on the lambrequin, and the lamp on the dark wood desk. Note how the latter functions as an end table, a practical note in this medium-sized bedroom where every inch of space was used to the ultimate. Across the room an open armchair picks up the lemon accent again; in combination with the small occasional table, it creates a corner for relaxation. Good looks, total comfort, a peaceful mood, and a dash of practicality are the keynotes of this charming room that works around the clock.

OVERLEAF An antique armoire, which can be dismantled into seven pieces, is used to divide this large-scale master bedroom into two distinct areas—one for sleeping, the other for dressing.

In the dressing area the armoire functions as a wardrobe. Shelves for pocketbooks, shoes, and sweaters have been built into the unit; hanging rods for blouses and shirts were installed in the upper section. Drawers provide extra space for lingerie. The armoire is positioned opposite a substantial walk-in closet (not shown). This is well fitted out to hold more clothes; a full-length mirror is attached to the inside of the closet door. Designer *Virginia Frankel,* A.S.I.D., designed this bedroom to serve as a dual-purpose space, incorporating the dressing area in the bedroom rather than closing it off in a hallway.

By using one color throughout for walls, floor, and ceiling, as well as for curtains and bedspread, the entire space appears enlarged through visual illusion; any imperfections and sharp angles are also camouflaged. The only other color used in addition to the mellow wood tones is in the decorative linen braid of parrot green and white, which trims the draperies, dust ruffle, and headboard.

The smart but simple window treatment combines fabrics of various weights, such as the heavy, tightly woven fabric of the draperies (also used on the walls) and the sheer linen casements. These gently filter light but ensure privacy. A collection of family photographs on the dressing-area wall provides a sentimental touch.

PRECEDING PAGES In the sleeping area the back of the armoire becomes a headboard for the king-sized bed. To duplicate the design of the curtains and dust ruffle, the armoire is upholstered with a shaped piece of foam rubber and covered in the same linen used to make the draperies. The trim is the identical green braid used on the dust ruffle and the window treatment.

The slim dressing table with recessed drawers runs the whole length of one wall in the bedroom. It is not only practical but highly decorative. A collection of personal accessories and family photographs are charmingly mingled together. Jewelry is hung from tiny hooks on the wall and looks like an art display. An antique mirror, an old lamp, and flowers add to the wallscape and also help to break up the long expanse of wall. Such things as the candelabrum on the headboard, the handsome ceiling-hung chandelier, and a collection of colorful throw pillows add to the decorative overtones of the tranquil and restful room.

The master bathroom, which is part of the dressing room area, can be seen in the background. A medley of pastel colors and a bright pink bathroom carpet provide sparks of color in this all-white cocoon. A storage area in the bathroom (not shown) was created by enclosing the washbasin in a plywood vanity and wallpapering the latter in the same paper as the walls.

This bed/sitting room utilizes a minimal amount of space to the best possible advantage. Designer *Virginia Perlo* created dual-purpose space on a shoestring budget by using only a few pieces of furniture, an amusing sheet pattern, and some imagination.

The impressionistic print of the sheet pattern is the nucleus for the room decor. The ready-made bedspread and the "bed curtains," which are really a double-size sheet, establish a luxurious, semicanopied air. The curtains were ceiling hung from a cornice made from solid-color sheeting in tangerine—selected from the tangerine, cocoa, and white in the print.

The curtain-and-cornice duo is carried over to the other wall to frame the writing desk. On this wall a matching laminated window shade keeps the decorative theme intact and the entire project within its budget. Do-it-yourself know-how and a sense of color and style can create a marvelous environment with almost no money at all. The traditional desk and chair blend harmoniously with the pattern and are small enough in scale to fit the small dimensions of this apartment bedroom. To create a sense of height and size, the pattern on the sheets has been installed vertically to direct your eyes away from the small, boxlike atmosphere that often exists in modern apartments.

Pull a Dining Room Out of Thin Air

Many modern apartments lack a separate dining room, as do smaller apartments in old buildings or converted brownstones. Yet everyone needs a place for family meals and entertaining. Providing such a spot may seem like an insurmountable problem to solve successfully.

However, there is no reason to be dismayed if you are faced with this task. It is possible to pull a dining area out of thin air through the clever utilization of space, imaginative and ingenious decorating, and the use of the right furnishings.

First analyze your entire apartment, paying particular attention to general living areas. By doing this you will be able to recognize and pinpoint appropriate areas that can be transformed for dining. Your main concern is naturally with space. Wherever the area is located in the apartment, it must be large enough to accommodate a dining table, several chairs and, if possible, a server, although the latter is not all that essential. When space is really at a premium, you can use a rolling cart to function as a serving piece and simply tuck it away in another area of the apartment, or in a closet, when it is not required for meals. A circular or square folding card table that can be stored easily is a possible alternative to a cart; an attractive tablecloth will hide its utilitarian appearance.

Areas that Can Be Transformed for Dining

There are many areas in even the most standard apartment where you can set up a comfortable spot for dining, whether intended only for family meals or for entertaining as well. Consider the following.

LIVING ROOM

Generally, this is the one room in an apartment with the most amount of space; it is obviously a convenient place to create a dining area. View the living room from all angles and select the most appropriate area. This might be in a corner, at one end, or in front of the windows. Allocate a given amount of space and measure it. Then go to a furniture store and investigate the dining room furniture available. Measure the pieces you prefer to make sure they are not too large for the area and will not intrude too much into the rest of the living room and make it look unbalanced.

Arrange the dining pieces in the most attractive way. Sometimes it's a good idea to place two chairs next to each other on the far side of the table, against a wall, or in front of the window. The two other chairs can then be placed at either end of the table, set at an angle and facing into the room. This type of grouping helps to make the dining pieces seem a little more integrated with the conversation area in the room. If possible, arrange the seating pieces in such a way that they create a self-contained look and, in so doing, help to demarcate the two specific areas within the overall space. For instance, a sofa that juts into the room, with its back facing the dining area, helps to create a sense of separateness without visually blocking out one end of the room. Two armchairs placed side by side, or with a small table in between, create the same effect. To repeat, although a serving piece is vital, it does not have to be included in the dining arrangement. However, an alternative to a rolling cart or folding table is a wall-hung shelf. This can be as narrow as nine inches, so it does not intrude too much into the space, and can be mounted onto a wall or become an extension of the window ledge if there is one. When a ledge does not exist, a shelf can be attached to the wall just under the window. The shelf can be of lacquered wood topped with heat-resistant glass or covered with plastic laminate. Thick glass can also be used for the shelf. Because of its transparency, it appears to take up little space.

DEN

Many people prefer to turn a spare room in an apartment into a den, study, or library. Certainly this type of general-purpose room is more useful in the long run than a dining room, which, after all, is only occupied at mealtimes. However, there is no reason why a den cannot be utilized for dining as well through a little clever decorating. For example, a Parsons table used as a desk can work as a dining table as well when required. Likewise, a glass dining table can function as a desk. Dining chairs can be of the folding type—made of plastic, Plexiglas, wood, or metal—which are easy to store in a closet or under a bed. A large, circular, unfinished wood table topped with a floor-length cloth can be situated in a corner of the den and used to display a lamp, accessories, and magazines. With the removal of these objects, the skirted table works beautifully as a dining table for four or six, depending on its size. There are also tables on the market that can be raised or lowered to different heights to suit specific needs. This type of table will function well as a coffee table placed in front of a sofa or easy chairs in a den. With a flip of a switch it can be raised to dining height to comfortably serve four or six guests, depending on its size.

Freestanding bookshelf/storage units, which are ideal to use in a den, often have a built-in table that flips down and extends into the room to become a dining table when required. The surface can work as a desk at other times.

FOYER

Depending on its size, a foyer or entrance hall can be transformed into an attractive dining area. You can furnish it to look like a dining room, with a table surrounded by chairs and a small console or server against a wall. Or, if space is at a premium, you can decorate it in such a way that it hides these mannerisms most of the time. Obviously, the size of the foyer limits the pieces you can include, but the only really essential items are a table and chairs. A rolling cart, a folding table, or a wall-hung shelf can be utilized as a server, and you can buy folding chairs that can be stored in a closet until they are needed.

A circular skirted table, a circular glass table, and a traditional wood table with extension leaves that can be added as required are all ideal to use in a foyer. The table should be placed in an appropriate spot and treated to a vase of flowers, a plant, or other accessories for an overall decorative look during the day. These are simple to remove at mealtimes. If you do not have enough space to position a table permanently, consider using a folding table that need only be set up when required.

Traffic lanes are important in any room in an apartment, but they are particularly crucial in a foyer or entrance, so do take them into consideration when arranging your furniture. People must be able to enter, leave, and move across a foyer without having to squeeze between pieces of furniture.

KITCHENS

Dining in the kitchen has become quite popular in the last few years for a variety of reasons. Not the least of these, of course, is lack of available dining space. However, a dining area included in the kitchen has certain advantages. It is an intimate and cozy environment for meals with the family or for entertaining, and it also enables the hostess-cook to be with her guests while attending to bubbling pots and pans.

The kind of dining area you create in a kitchen naturally depends on the amount of space available. If you are lucky enough to occupy an old-fashioned apartment that has lots of kitchen space, you can set up a charming dining area at one end. This can be complete with sideboard, hutch, or any other types of serving pieces, in addition to the standard table and chairs.

When space is a little more limited, ingenuity and clever decorating are in order. For example, you can create a dining corner at one end of the room by utilizing built-in banquettes and a drop-leaf table. The banquettes should be made of wood, with hinged tops that lift up. The interior space can be used for storing large items or linen. Seating and back pads or large, loose cushions must be added for total comfort. A drop-leaf table will fit neatly into the area and will take up little space when pushed close to the banquettes. When dining it is just pulled out and its leaves are lifted to accommodate the diners. Folding chairs are a useful addition when more guests have to be catered to at different times. Simply arrange them at the other end of the table facing the banquettes. Incidentally, banquettes can be built in other rooms as well to create a cozy dining area, as will be discussed later in this chapter.

A counter attached to a wall and serviced by tall stools or chairs provides comfortable dining space in a minuscule kitchen. When the dimensions are really confined, you can use a hinged shelf that drops down flat against the wall when not required for meals, serviced by stacking stools that are stored in a closet during those busy working hours in the kitchen. A peninsula that extends into the kitchen is basically a food-preparation surface, but it can also double as a dining counter when partnered with tall stools or chairs.

Selecting Appropriate Furniture

When you are creating a dining area within a room that serves another function, you should pay strict attention to the furniture you choose. Dining pieces must blend with the other items situated elsewhere in the space to achieve a sense of style and total coordination. They should underscore the overall decorative mood created by the existing pieces and should not in any way compete or create an unharmonious feeling.

If you are creating a dining area in a living room or den, be certain that the dining pieces are of the same style and period as the furniture already in the room. For example, if the ambience is traditional, select a traditional table and chairs for true compatibility between the two areas. When the mood of a room is contemporary, pick out a modern dining table and chairs for a smooth, flowing look throughout, one that reiterates the basic style.

Occasionally you can digress from this rule if you want to produce a slightly eclectic look. For instance, you can select a simply styled, sleek-lined, steel-and-glass table for a traditionally decorated room. This type of table works because the steel and glass do not compete with the wood tones elsewhere; the streamlined style of the table does not detract from the more elaborate styling of the period pieces. But you should balance the table with traditional chairs. By the same token, you can sometimes include a traditional wood table in a contemporary setting, providing the style is clean in line and not too ornate. Partner it with modern chairs that blend in and are in step with the total decorative theme.

Always pay attention to wood tones. Too many different woods in a room produce a busy effect and detract from the smooth look you are trying to achieve. This is so because varied woods halt the eye, are often jarring and, of course, compete with each other.

If you choose dining room furniture made of other materials, such as cane, wicker, Plexiglas, plastic, or wrought iron, make sure that at least one piece made of the same material is situated in another part of the room. Upholstered dining chairs should not be covered with fabric that clashes with other fabrics on seating pieces or in draperies. They must either match the color and pattern used elsewhere in the room or, alternatively, achieve a coordinated effect.

These same points apply to dining areas you are creating in foyers, entrance halls, and kitchens.

Furniture that Saves Space

Today it is possible to purchase all kinds of furniture that saves space. Before making your final decision, it's a good idea to visit large furniture and department stores to view all the latest pieces on the market.

WALL-HUNG FURNITURE

Obviously this is a great space saver since it utilizes the walls and so frees the floor for other pieces; it also allows for good traffic patterns. Total wall systems can be purchased that include shelves, storage cabinets, counter space, and drop-leaf tables that work well for dining purposes. These systems come in a variety of wood tones and other materials. Styling runs the gamut from modern to traditional, thus enabling you to fulfill a decorative mood most successfully. *Freestanding systems* and *modular case pieces* have basically the same characteristics and work in the same way as wall-hung furniture. The only difference is that these pieces are simply placed against the wall and not hung on it. This is an important point to bear in mind, since you avoid costly installation and the furniture is easy to dismantle and take with you should you decide to relocate.

LIGHTLY SCALED FURNITURE

Many furniture manufacturers, conscious of the space problems we all face today, have designed and produced furniture specially scaled to fit into smaller rooms in apartments. For example, dining tables, chairs, servers, sideboards, hutches, and consoles are being made in smaller sizes so as to take up as little floor space as possible and match the scaled-down dimensions of many modern rooms. These pieces are available in both contemporary and traditional designs to suit individual tastes.

SPACE-SAVING MATERIALS

Certain materials are perfect for use in limited space because they appear to take up little room thanks to visual illusion. Glass combined with chrome, steel, brass, or light-colored wood is the most obvious choice. Because of its see-through qualities, glass does not stop the eye and so opens up an area and introduces an airy look. Tables, étagères, consoles, and rolling carts made of glass should be considered if you have real space problems to contend with.

Light wood tones, wood painted or lacquered a light color, cane, wicker, and white-painted wrought iron are other materials that help to introduce a more spacious feeling in a small room or limited area. This is so because these materials are light in appearance—pieces made from them are generally light in scale as well—and thus produce an airy look.

Always bear in mind that materials with a see-through quality or shiny surface and those of a neutral color or painted a light tone all tend to recede and so visually appear to take up little space. Dark wood tones or other materials painted a dark or very bright color seem to advance and, in so doing, look as if they are taking up more space than is actually the case. Select materials carefully to achieve the best possible effect.

Practical Ways to Divide

When you are creating a dining area at one end of a living room, it is sometimes possible to actually divide the room into two separate sections for specific activities, say, for dining and general relaxation.

There are many ways to demarcate space. You can do it by arranging your living room furniture in such a way that it creates a self-contained look in one portion of the room.

A library table, Parsons table, or console jutting out into the room between dining and living areas is another good way to divide a room at a low level without visually blocking out one section. A chest or cabinet finished on both sides can be positioned in the same way to achieve the same effect, as can a desk and matching chair.

Two chrome-and-glass étagères positioned in the same spot on opposite walls so that they protrude into the room is another interesting way to cut a room in half. Because of the see-through quality of the glass, both areas can easily be seen without creating a sense of confinement in either. Decorative objects and plants arranged on the shelves add lots of visual interest.

Freestanding or modular units, particularly those with base storage cabinets topped by shelves, can be utilized to demarcate an area. The open shelves permit both sections to be viewed easily and, again, accessories, books, and plants placed on the shelves introduce additional decorative overtones.

Gates made of wood or metal can be hung on two facing walls at the exact point in the room where you wish to create a sense of division. They should not meet and close in the center of the room, an effect that would be too overpowering. Instead, they should be left open and folded back to create the illusion of two separate areas without blocking one's view or any traffic lanes.

An arrangement of plants and small trees positioned between the two different areas within the room is another way to skillfully divide a space without creating a confined look in either section. Plants should be of varying heights and types to introduce a sense of movement and a play of different greens. A truly interesting effect of light and shadow is produced when small spotlights are positioned on the floor among the plants, with the light directed to the ceiling.

A window makes an ideal spot to create a dining area. Designer/painter *Renee Feinstein* made an old-fashioned window the focal point of one wall in a small living room, adding dining pieces that cater to leisurely meals. Color was her catalyst. She painted the walls a vivid green and then added a taupe shade finished with red and green trimming. The shade, which is in harmony with the contemporary furnishings, provides filtered light by day and privacy by night. The sill-hugging drop-leaf table slims down to a mere nine inches when closed. It is partnered with matching wood chairs that can be stacked and stored when not required. An étagère filled with plants doubles as a server when required. More plants adorn the window sill for an additional decorative touch.

In another variation on the same theme, designer *Michael Sherman* transformed the corner of a living room into a delightful dining area with a character all its own. A surprising combination of deep anemone walls with white shade cloth-covered vertical blinds establishes the color scheme. The slats of the textured shades add a fresh, sunlit mood that is stunning against the dark walls. The oblong table, which seats four, is a perfect size for the area. It is coupled with pewter-and-cane chairs that share the same see-through quality of the window treatment. Small in scale, they appear to take up little space. The glass-topped server, also lightly scaled, doubles as a room divider. As the designer has pointed out, it is relatively easy to dine elegantly in the tiniest of areas if furniture and accessories have been chosen with care.

OVERLEAF The bachelor who occupies this apartment wanted a dining area for more formal meals and entertaining rather than a makeshift snack corner. Because the living room was relatively small, interior designer *Emy Leeser* paid great attention to dividing the space carefully to include a permanent dining setup at one end of the room. She used a variety of ideas to control and demarcate space effectively and to create the right ambience. She dispensed with the idea of a room divider, which would have created a confined effect and blocked out light. Instead she used several visual aids to pinpoint the two specific areas within the room. The clever placement of furniture and wall-hung pieces were other key factors in the successful decoration of this room, which works on two levels. The designer began by lining the two main walls of the living area with natural-toned Belgian linen; the third window wall (not visible) was treated to Belgian linen casements to permit natural daylight to flow in yet also preserve some degree of privacy. The fabric on the walls was carried along the beam in the dining area to give the effect of an alcove. The two walls in this area were painted bright orange and then treated to wall-hung furniture. The shelves, filled with books and accessories, make a decorative statement while freeing floor space. In combination with the orange walls they help to create an enclosed, intimate feeling; they also demarcate the area from the living room. Again to save space the designer selected long benches to service the butcher block dining table, rather than chairs, which would have been too cumbersome. The benches are topped with orange velvet seating pads. Illumination at this end of the room is provided by a modern ceiling fixture. A rolling cart (not shown) acts as a server, and is stowed away in a closet when not needed. Six can be comfortably seated at the table; when eight are being entertained, the table and benches can be pulled out to permit the inclusion of two folding director's chairs at either end. For total continuity of wood tones and colors *Emy Leeser* used orange cushions on the brown velvet modular seating pieces, along with a butcher block coffee table that echoes the one in the dining area.

PRECEDING PAGES In this second photo of the living room you can see how clever placement of the seating pieces creates a sense of demarcation without visually blocking out light. Both areas are, in effect, quite self-contained yet in harmony with each other through the repetition of colors, fabrics, and wood tones. The long unit was selected as a perfect storage piece; it is also ideal as an additional server when required. A matching wall-hung cabinet that holds china and crystal is another space-saving idea. The platform in front of the window, covered in Belgian linen, is a practical unit for displaying a hi-fi, records, and plants.

When you are stuck without a dining room or sufficient space to create one in a living room, consider using a large-sized coffee table for meals, impromptu or otherwise. Providing the table is large enough, you can entertain just as elegantly in the living room if you choose tabletop items carefully and with an eye to aesthetics. This charming coffee table setting shows just how it's done. A blue and white tablecloth, chosen to echo the blue and white color scheme of the room, makes the perfect backdrop for white china and crystal in this setting for four, complete with candles and flowers. Low couches and ottomans service the table à la japonaise.

Rembrandt

This second coffee table setting was planned for buffet-style dining in a living room lacking a corner where dining pieces could be included. The large glass table, supported by a wood base, is sufficient for all that is required. Dining can be planned in a jiffy and without much fuss. Several cane occasional tables (only one is visible) hold such things as bread, fruit, and a coffee service. The coffee table is just the right height for the low sofas that surround it.

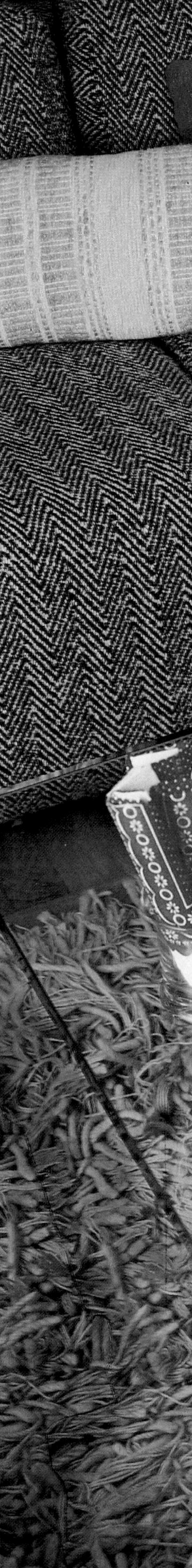

Sometimes a foyer is large enough to serve as a dining area, as illustrated here. Interior designer *Jane Victor* introduced elegant overtones and dispensed with foyer mannerisms by using panels of hand-painted fabric on all the walls. This black and white print accented with terracotta is decorated with Egyptian motifs. The panels of fabric were framed with molding. Each is intersected by narrow columns running from floor to ceiling that bear hand-painted Egyptian designs. The wall treatment creates the effect of a total room rather than an entrance and also repeats the decorative mood of the adjoining living room, thus creating a real feeling of continuity. A white flokati area rug acts as the anchor for the dining pieces, which consist of an unfinished wood table skirted in gray felt and modern black-and-chrome chairs. A handsome antique chandelier introduces a further touch of elegance, while plants and a sculpture on a Plexiglas table add final decorative touches. The chairs can be moved back against various walls when not needed for dining to allow for proper traffic patterns. The table remains stationary at all times and can be used to hold flowers, magazines, and books. *Jane Victor* suggests the following alternate furniture if cost or space problems are a consideration: a circular folding card table and folding chairs that can be stored in a closet and set out when formal dining is a must.

Although this modern apartment did not have a dining room, there was ample space in the large living room to create a spot for dining—and a comfortable and attractive one at that. The owners wanted to create two quite distinct areas, each with a feeling of self-contained separateness, without spoiling the flow of space throughout the entire room. To this end they used the simple device of a divider. The divider actually consists of several freestanding units composed of base storage cabinets richly finished on both sides, plus chrome-and-glass shelves. In combination they provide space for displaying accessories, hi-fi equipment, and interior storage—and the end unit doubles as a server. Skillful placement of the armchair, which, like the other living room furniture, matches the dining set, also help to demarcate the dining area from the conversation area. The glass dining table, with a rosewoodlike insert in the center, is combined with four chrome-framed chairs upholstered in a super-soft kidlike urethane fabric. Both the table and chairs have a light-as-air look to them and appear to take up less space because of their scale. By using furniture and colors that match, a sense of unity is established between the two areas.

The owners of this brownstone basement apartment were faced with the problem of a large living room having to serve a variety of living needs, including cooking and dining as well as relaxation. Rather than doing an extensive and costly remodeling job to create a kitchen and dining room, they decided to use an open floor plan to provide these facilities. They built a kitchen area at one end of the room next to a series of closets; it included all the equipment that was needed, from a large refrigerator to an oven and dishwasher. All were aligned along two walls. They then built an L-shaped peninsula that fronts the kitchen area and serves not only as work space but also as a spot for dining. Storage is provided in the base of the peninsula on the kitchen side. The dining counter, serviced by tall wooden chairs, also doubles as a bar when required. Plenty of good illumination is provided by droplights suspended from the ceiling. The beauty of this open planning is that it permits the hostess to be part of the general entertaining while preparing food. The sleek lines of the peninsula and the chairs blend well with the contemporary decor of the living area, which is based on a play of gold and brown. Nylon carpeting was used throughout because of its durability and ease of maintenance.

PRECEDING PAGES When *Pat McMillan* was asked to decorate this apartment living room, one of the problems she had to solve was creating a dining area within its limited boundaries. Since the room was relatively small, she wanted to avoid a crowded look. Her solution was to cover one wall with a mirror. This helps to create an illusion of more space and gives the dining area a floating, airy look. Underscoring this visual illusion is the furniture. The designer used a chrome-and-glass table and chrome-and-canvas chairs that appear to take up no space at all because of their see-through qualities and shiny surfaces. The étagère to one side of the table has the same effect. Note how the dining pieces echo the coffee table in the conversation area. All of these items consist of consumer-assembled furniture that you can purchase, transport, and put together yourself. The color scheme of white and beige accented with brown underscores the spacious ambience, as does the use of thin-slatted blinds at the window.

This second photo of the living room shows you how well the dining area blends in with the conversation area. In the far corner is the kitchen, where blinds matching those at the window have been used to create a unified look. To the side of the clock, a unique modern piece, is a wine rack that also doubles as a stand for the TV set, which can be swung around for viewing from the conversation area.

Here is another version of a dining table built into a modular unit. Although this one remains stationary at all times, it actually doubles as a desk when not used for dining. As you can see, it takes up little space and solves meal problems in cramped quarters. It services four or six with ease and can also be used for buffet entertaining. A spacious shelf against the wall provides an extra surface for candles and other dining utensils.

OVERLEAF In this era of space consciousness, dining in the kitchen has become extremely popular. All you need is enough space for a table and four or six chairs. In this charming candy-colored kitchen, space was not a problem, since there had been some extensive remodeling done. The long, narrow kitchen in this turn-of-the-century apartment building had been joined to a small room adjacent to it through the simple removal of a wall. The extra space was utilized for dining through the inclusion of a circular wood table and four white plastic chairs. The pink and white checked cloth and the yellow china echo the pink-yellow-white-and-green checked wall covering covered with flowers. These same colors appear in the narrow-slatted blind at the window; the yellow and white vinyl floor repeats the colors of the cabinets and counter tops. Designer *Virginia Frankel,* A.S.I.D., used some other decorative touches to give the kitchen pretty overtones for dining. These include the use of wall covering on the front of the dishwasher; a collection of attractive accessories; plants in the window area and on the plastic stacking tables. A low-hanging globe-shaped lighting fixture provides illumination over the dining table. The designer has pointed out that there is enough space to include a second table for four when eight guests are being entertained. A circular card table or an unfinished wood circular top on a metal tripod base —both of which can be stored away easily—would be ideal. Either would be perfect with folding or stacking chairs.

The Forsyte Saga
THE LOCKWOOD CONCERN
A NOVEL BY

This handsome drop-leaf table in the Georgian style fits neatly into one end of a living room. Representing a beautiful reproduction of an antique piece, it is diminutive with the leaves down (measuring only 22½″×47″) and makes a perfect console against a wall. With the leaves up it serves four quite adequately; when three fillers are used it can comfortably seat eight. Fitted with casters, the cherry wood table can be moved around easily. If necessary, it can be used in the foyer as a console and need only be rolled into the living room when required. Here it is shown with host and hostess armchairs upholstered in a flame-stitch fabric, but it can be partnered with any type of traditional chair—or even a modern one if you want to create an eclectic ambience.

Freestanding modular units are a boon for apartment living, since they save a great deal of space by utilizing walls while providing all manner of facilities. As often as not a dining table is built in. This table disappears from sight when not required; the chrome legs flip up under the table, which then slides back into the unit. Partnered here with two chrome-framed chairs, the table seats four easily.

americana
second chance

This small area adjoining a living room in a New York City apartment was far too tiny to be used as a self-contained dining room with formal dining room furniture. However, interior designer *Lois Munroe Hoyt,* A.S.I.D., used skill and ingenuity to turn it into a charming spot for dining. She began her decorating scheme—which came to less than four hundred dollars—by lining the walls with mirror tiles to create a feeling of greater space and to open up the area. She covered the floor with twelve-inch square self-stick vinyl floor tiles that are easy to put down yourself. In combination with the floor, the white-painted shutters and other woodwork create a sense of airiness. With the shell in place, the designer then had hinged banquettes—that double as storage boxes—made out of plywood. They are upholstered in foam rubber and covered with a green and white fabric. Foam rubber pads covered in the same fabric serve as backrests to provide extra comfort while dining. The old-fashioned wood table, which fits neatly into the area, was lacquered white to give it a brand-new look. Two Queen Anne side chairs were lacquered spring green and upholstered in the same green and white fabric. In combination with the banquettes, they permit six to dine comfortably. Incidentally, since the banquettes reach to the floor, the designer protected the bases with self-stick floor tiles left over from the floor, which she cut to make a four-inch border. This budget decorating job turned the 6½′×8′ space into a modern, easy-care dining area filled with spring freshness the year round.

4

Revamps for Standard Kitchens and Bathrooms

Kitchens and bathrooms are often the most architecturally uninteresting rooms in an apartment. Though they appear to defy really good decoration, this need not always be the case. It is certainly no longer necessary to put up with the look of yesterday or the dullness of standard modern design.

Kitchens

These fall into various categories such as small, squared off, and bland; galleylike and too narrow; or old-fashioned and impractical. However, it is possible to introduce a fresh new look into all of these different types of kitchens, regardless of their size, through a little ingenious revamping and clever decorating. By utilizing a variety of new products and materials, it is relatively easy to revamp these areas on a reasonable budget without going to the expense of total remodeling. Let's take a look at several elements that can help you accomplish this.

How to Add Decorative Flair

Style, decorative flair, and good looks can be introduced into any kitchen through the use of attractive wall coverings, paint, and accessories. A wide range of these products is available today at moderate cost. This is a vital consideration if you are working on a limited budget. The things you choose will depend on your personal taste, the look you want to produce and, to a certain extent, the size of the kitchen.

WALL COVERINGS

Undoubtedly the best buy today is vinyl wall covering. For one thing, it is reasonably priced. Aside from this, it is also extremely hard-wearing, soil-and-stain resistant, moisture resistant, easy to keep clean with soap-and-water sponging, and comes in designer colors and delightful patterns. Not only that, it is easy to put up yourself, since it is pretrimmed and strippable. Some vinyls are also prepasted, which makes your task that much easier.

Before selecting a vinyl or, for that matter, any other wall covering, consider the size of the kitchen and the amount of free wall space you need to cover. If the kitchen is small, pay attention to pattern and color. Large, oversized patterns can overwhelm a small space, and since bright or dark colors appear to advance, they tend to reduce the feeling of space quite a lot. Your best bet, in this instance, are patterns that are small in scale, open, and airy; colors should be fresh and light in tone. These will help the kitchen to look bigger. If your kitchen is large, then you can be a little more venturesome and select a bold pattern and vivid colors.

The pattern you choose should be determined by the overall decorative mood you wish to create. For instance, if you want an old-fashioned country feeling, then look at such traditional patterns as florals, stripes, florals and stripes in combination, fruit or vegetable designs, or designs that simulate tiles, such as delft and mediterranean. A contemporary mood is reinforced through the use of abstract designs; trellis or lattice patterns; or fruit, vegetables, and florals depicted in a stylized, modern manner.

Generally a wall covering dictates a color scheme and, in fact, can act as a good color guide for keying the other colors to be used in the kitchen. When space is at a premium, it's wise to pick a light shade from the wall covering and use this for painted surfaces, floors, and kitchen equipment. In a larger space you can select something more vivid or unusual, keying the other elements to this shade. It's worth pointing out that too many colors in any room tend to introduce a busy look. For this reason select only *one* color from the wall covering and use it throughout.

Incidentally, many vinyl wall coverings come with a coordinated or matching fabric. When this is the case, use the matching fabric for window curtains or have the fabric laminated to a window shade. This matching up of walls and window helps to produce a custom-designed look. Another way to create this ambience and, at the same time, make the kitchen look larger is to use the wall covering on the ceiling and on the backs of doors. This is especially important in a small kitchen with little wall space or walls covered with cabinets and equipment. By distributing the vinyl throughout you can create a more decorative ambience.

Other wall coverings suitable for use in a kitchen are ceramic and metal tiles. Obviously these are more costly and must be installed by a professional, which adds to the total expense. Depending on their pattern, ceramic tiles can introduce a traditional or contemporary feeling; metal tiles tend to introduce a very modern look, which can sometimes appear very sterile and cold. However, both types of tiles are hard-wearing, soil-and-moisture-resistant, and are easy to clean with soap and water. Obviously tiles can only be used on the walls, so be sure to introduce a coordinated look throughout by painting the ceiling and door in a color that blends in with the tiles.

PAINT AND LACQUERS

Paint, that good old standby, is still very popular and practical for use in a kitchen. The same rules just mentioned apply when selecting a paint color. Light colors tend to recede, push walls out, and help to increase the feeling of space; dark or vivid colors seem to advance and reduce the feeling of spaciousness by visual illusion. So pick a paint color that helps correct space problems and underscores the mood you are trying to achieve. Most of the paints available today are durable and easy to sponge clean. If you want to create a slightly more glamorous look in your kitchen but prefer to stay with a solid-color painted background rather than a more decorative one, consider using lacquer. Lacquers in every conceivable color are readily available today. Because of the glossy finish they produce, they tend to create a more sophisticated ambience. Incidentally, the shiny surface of lacquer reflects light and bounces it back into the room, helping to create a sense of greater spaciousness by means of visual illusion.

Whether you select a standard paint or a lacquer, use it on the ceiling, on all woodwork trim, and on the door to create a unified effect throughout. Old metal cabinets and cupboards can also be revamped with the same paint or lacquer. Good wood cabinets should be left as they are, unless you prefer to paint them the color of the walls.

ACCESSORIES

A kitchen should be just as well accessorized as any other room in your apartment. Today you can introduce the most delightful effects through careful selection.

The type of accessories you select depends on the style of the kitchen and the amount of space you have to display them. If your kitchen is traditional or country/rustic in mood, consider using the following lovely old items to enhance this look. Copper molds, old-fashioned utensils, and cookware can be hung on the kitchen walls to make a definitive statement, as can pieces of ceramic, china plates, milk glass, and pewter objects. These can be displayed on wall-hung shelves. Old-fashioned kitchen prints or recipes are highly decorative —and don't forget plants. These work well in any kitchen and can be ceiling-hung, held by brackets attached to the wall, or suspended in front of the window. A rack of spices displayed in attractive bottles is both practical and pretty, as are staple items held in containers lined up on a counter.

Select modern accessories for a contemporary kitchen. All manner of accessories are available today. You can introduce a decorative effect by mingling them together. For instance, glass containers with cork stoppers come in all sizes and shapes. They are designed to hold such things as spaghetti, rice, dried fruits, and all types of staples. Line them up on a counter top or display them on wall-hung shelves. Modern spice racks are available, as are all kinds of modern cookware. Select pots and pans of modern design—they generally come in copper, stainless steel, or brightly enameled iron—and hang them on the wall so that they can be viewed at all times. Modern prints, graphics, and plants help to underscore the overall decorative theme in a contemporary kitchen.

A word of advice. If the kitchen is small, be highly selective. Don't buy too many accessories, as this tends to introduce an overcrowded, cluttered look that can seem messy or even haphazard. This rule applies equally to a traditional or modern kitchen.

Make Walls Work Overtime

Wall space in a kitchen is extremely important and should be carefully planned to make the most use of it. Cabinets will obviously take up some of the wall space, but the remaining space can be utilized to great advantage.

Look analytically at all the free wall space in your kitchen and then plan each section carefully. If you have a relatively large piece of wall space available, you can add extra cabinets if you need them. Otherwise think of adding shelves. These can be fairly narrow so they don't protrude too much. They are ideal for housing spices, staples, china, glass, accessories, and all manner of items. Put those items in constant use within easy reach.

The shelves can be of wood left in its natural state, painted, or of glass. How many shelves you are able to include of course depends on the size of the available piece of wall.

Alternatively, you can hang a large piece of pegboard instead of shelves. The hooks you attach will hold cooking utensils, small pots and pans, other items in everyday use, and perhaps an attractive wall print to add to the overall decorativeness. Paint the pegboard a bright color or contrast the color to the walls.

A small piece of wall can be treated to a wrought iron pot rack from which you can hang pots and pans. Old-fashioned in design and harking back to your great-grandmother's day, this item is very popular at the moment. Many manufacturers are making reproductions of these antique pot racks. Generally the wrought iron is painted black, although some modern designs come in copper or stainless steel. The pot racks consist of eight straight or slightly curved bars extending out from the wall so that pots and pans can be properly hung. In passing, it's worth mentioning that other old-fashioned pot racks that can be suspended from the ceiling are also available today. These, too, are usually reproductions.

A small piece of corner wall space can be given a corner cupboard or corner shelves for housing china, crystal, or other items. Either solution makes use of awkward corner space that might otherwise be wasted. Likewise, a bit of space between an end wall and a piece of kitchen equipment can be fitted out with a wine rack that fits into the little niche. There are several types of wine racks that can be wall-hung; however, be sure this job is done by a carpenter, as the wall must be properly plugged to take the weight of the wine rack and the bottles of wine or liquor.

How to Gain Extra Storage Space and Work Surfaces

With a little ingenuity it is possible to gain extra storage space and additional work surfaces in a kitchen that is short on both. Let's take a look at the techniques and products that help you to do this successfully.

STORAGE

Perhaps the easiest and cheapest way to introduce extra storage space into your kitchen is to utilize the backs of doors. Today several leading manufacturers of kitchen products are making all manner of plastic holders that can be attached to the insides of doors either with screws or a strong adhesive. By making use of the insides of doors, cupboard and cabinet space is freed for extra items. For example, you can get double use out of that cupboard under the sink where kitchen cleaning utensils and products are generally housed. There are small and large caddies for housing all of these, as well as holders for paper towels, food wrapping paper, and the like. There are large plastic lazy Susans available that can be used in this same cupboard for all manner of items.

You can increase the usefulness of a broom closet by attaching a plastic broom-and-mop holder on the back wall or inside the door. This plastic rack comes with hooks on which the handles, usually with holes, are hung, so that the brooms are suspended above the floor. This leaves plenty of room in the closet itself for other items.

A set of plastic sliding shelves fits neatly into the standard base cabinet. The lower shelf, which is on a metal runner, is attached to the bottom of the cupboard with screws. The shelves slide out to permit easy access to items being stored. Space in the cupboard is actually doubled. Pans can be stacked on the lower shelf and pots and large items on the top shelf.

Two-tiered lazy Susans, also made of plastic, allow you to house twice as much in the average cabinet. They can be utilized for spices, staples, plates, cups, and saucers. Some of them come with hooks so that cups and mugs can be hung. Plate racks permit you to store more than the usual amount of china in a standard cabinet, protect the plates from chipping, and let you see at a glance exactly what is where.

Another type of plastic holder is designed to accommodate an ironing board. This holder is screwed onto the back of a closet door and the ironing board is simply hung onto it. The holder is topped with a caddy for miscellaneous items. Matching caddies store shopping bags, garbage bags, and similar items. All these products are a boon in any kitchen, regardless of whether or not storage space is at a premium. They are inexpensive to purchase and are available at department stores and houseware stores across the country.

WORK SURFACES

Many kitchens lack adequate counter space. This can be a tough problem to solve, particularly when there is literally no space to add extra counter tops. If you are faced with this problem, scrutinize your kitchen carefully. Chances are you will find a spot where an extra counter, however small, can be added. Sometimes there is a bit of available space in a window area above a radiator. A piece of wood, topped with plastic laminate, can often be attached to the window ledge, extending it so that it provides a spot for preparing vegetables. When there is no radiator under the window, you can use a hinged shelf that drops down flat against the wall when not in use. The same type of hinged shelf can be attached to a piece of spare wall to work as a counter top when needed. This practical idea is especially useful in a kitchen where space is really tight, such as a narrow, galleylike kitchen.

A chopping board with variable-length handles that extend over the sides of the sink is ideal for providing that extra solid surface for food preparation. This kind of chopping board, generally made of butcher block wood, can be purchased at some houseware and department stores for under ten dollars.

In an old-fashioned kitchen where equipment such as a refrigerator and a dishwasher are not set flush against each other, there is often a bit of space between them. Have a piece of wood topped with plastic laminate, or butcher block wood, fitted into the space. Even if the amount of space is very small, it is still worthwhile, since it provides a counter top for canisters, trays, and other items; in so doing it frees a larger surface for working with food.

When floor space is not all that confined, you can use a drop-leaf table to act as a counter or, alternatively, a butcher block chopping board that comes with legs and fits neatly into a corner. If none of these ideas are suitable because of space limitations, as a last resort you can purchase a small folding table that stores flat and can be set up only when you are really pressed for additional counter surface, perhaps when you are catering to a large number of guests and have lots of food to prepare.

Practical Products for Floors

The type of product you use on the kitchen floor depends on several things: personal taste, the decorative look you wish to create, and the amount of money you have to spend.

To my mind, **vinyl** is still one of the best buys around. It comes in sheets or tiles and is the most popular type of resilient flooring. It is easy to clean and maintains a sheen without waxing. Vinyl wears extremely well and is highly resilient; all vinyls resist grease, abrasion, acid, and bleach. Apart from its great durability, vinyl comes in a wide range of colors; patterns and designs run the gamut from modern to traditional. Great decorative effects can be created with vinyl.

Rubber tile is another distinctive flooring popular in kitchens. It is a little costlier than other resilient floor coverings, but it has certain advantages. It is nonporous, flexible, and stainproof. Apart from its natural resilience, which cushions footsteps and absorbs sound, it is slip-resistant, easy to maintain, and durable. Rubber tiles are usually available in a marblelike design and come in a variety of colors.

Ceramic tiles work well in a kitchen. However, they are more expensive than the two previously mentioned floor coverings. Ceramic tiles come in either a glazed or unglazed finish. Both work well on floors, but it is the unglazed type that is the most popular. Both have hard, nonporous surfaces. Unglazed ceramic tile is produced in a variety of earth colors; the glazed kind is available in an even wider selection of colors. Its durability, ease of maintenance, and unlimited design possibilities make ceramic tile an ideal flooring in kitchens of all types.

Carpeting can also be used in a kitchen. The best type to select is an indoor/outdoor carpet made of polypropylene olefin. This fiber is comparable to nylon in abrasion resistance and strength, but it is less resilient than nylon. It has a low rate of water absorption. This makes cleaning easy. It also resists acids and bleaching. Because of the density and stain repellency of polypropylene olefin carpets, they are popular for kitchens as well as the outdoors. Naturally, carpeting does add comfort underfoot and introduces a luxurious touch, but make sure you buy the right type. Polypropylene olefin comes in a variety of colors and patterns, enabling you to introduce a highly decorative effect on the floor.

Whichever product you select for your kitchen floor, it should underscore the general mood created by the basic color scheme and wall covering.

Window Treatments

Kitchen windows in apartments are usually not very large. Their treatment must consequently be planned carefully. Here are some treatments that work successfully.

Window shades are ideal. They are unobtrusive, fit neatly into the frame, are easy to manipulate, permit natural daylight to flow, and are highly decorative. You can select a solid-color shade and trim it with borders of stick-on braid, decals, cutouts of the wall covering used, or stenciled designs if you are a do-it-yourselfer with a bent for painting. Alternatively, a window shade can be laminated with a fabric that matches the wall covering to create a custom-designed look. It is not necessary to add a valance unless this is your personal preference.

Vertical blinds work well in any kitchen, particularly in one of contemporary design. The vertical slats, usually made of shade cloth, are neat and clean-lined, fitting easily within the window's frame. They introduce light control and privacy when required.

If you have designed a country kitchen, you should consider **louvered shutters** for the window, as this type of treatment helps to underscore the basic theme. Leading manufacturers of shutters are making them in a number of sizes to fit standard apartment windows. They come in an unfinished state that you can stain or paint the color of your choice to blend in with the overall color scheme.

An alternative treatment for a rustic-style kitchen is a set of **cafe curtains**, preferably made of a fabric matching the wall covering or one that is coordinated with it. Cafe curtains are usually hung on rods and can be double- or triple-tiered, depending on the size of the window. When you use three tiers, remember that the top one should be narrow, in a sense serving as a valance.

Select a fabric that is easy to launder, as cafe curtains and other types used in a kitchen do tend to collect dust and grease over a period of time.

Narrow-slatted blinds, an updated version of venetian blinds, have become increasingly popular for kitchen windows in the last few years because they have a slick, modern look and come in a wide range of colors, or combination of colors, to create unique striped effects. They provide light control, privacy, and are easy to clean. Like the other blinds mentioned, they fit neatly within the frame and are not obtrusive while being highly decorative.

Lighting Ideas

Many apartment kitchens lack a window, so obviously artificial illumination is of great importance. In point of fact, even if you do have one or more windows, lighting is still vital and should be well planned.

The basic lighting requirements in a kitchen are as follows:

1. You should provide for overhead illumination that spreads light over the entire area. This can be in the form of strip lighting, a single fixture with strong bulbs, or a contemporary or traditional chandelier, depending on the style of the kitchen.

2. The overhead fixture should be reinforced with spot lighting in areas where certain activities take place; this is especially important if the kitchen is large. Food preparation centers and the cooking area should be well illuminated to avoid accidents. If there is space between the wall-hung cabinets and the counter tops, consider adding strip lighting under the cabinets. This is an ideal way to illuminate the surface where food is being prepared. Fixtures are relatively inexpensive and easy to install yourself. A hood placed over a range generally comes fitted with a light, so that you can easily view pots and pans and thereby avoid accidents.

3. If you are including a dining area within the kitchen, be sure to plan lighting for this spot. You can use a ceiling-hung fixture that drops down low over the table or, alternatively, wall fixtures that swivel around to produce the best results. Candles look pretty for dining; you should use them on the table if this

suits your taste. However, don't rely on candles alone for lighting the dining area within a kitchen.

4. Select fixtures, strip lighting, and bulbs with care to produce the best effect. Remember, very harsh lighting can become tiring and also creates a cold, unattractive mood. On the other hand, dull lighting introduces a gloomy mood that is not conducive to working or dining. You should endeavor to create a mixture of bright and warm, soft light for total convenience and comfort.

Bathrooms

Most apartment bathrooms are squared-off boxes lacking adequate space and totally without personality. Just as you can update kitchens with a little revamping, you can create a new mood in a bathroom. Today there are lots of good products available that enable you to do this easily and on a medium budget. Revamping is your best solution; remodeling can cost a fortune and this kind of expenditure is hardly worth it if you are renting.

Create a New Ambience

It is possible to create a fresh, new ambience in any bathroom through a little skillful decorating, selectively choosing products for walls and floor, picking linens that add color and luxury, and, of course, assembling the right accessories. Here are a few guidelines.

WALLS

Most walls in an apartment bathroom are partially covered with tiles. Although this would seem to make them doubly difficult to decorate effectively, this is not so. You can achieve stunning effects by literally ignoring the tiles and decorating the other portions of the walls, as well as the ceiling and the door.

Unlike a kitchen, a bathroom is not occupied around the clock, so you can afford to be a little more daring and dramatic with wall coverings, color schemes, and patterns. Even in the smallest of bathrooms you can use vivid or strong colors and dominant patterns or designs because they are not being constantly viewed and therefore don't become overpowering or boring.

WALL COVERINGS

The same kind of vinyl wall covering intended for kitchens is also available for use in bathrooms—in more appropriate patterns, of course. Vinyl is perfect for a bath since it is moisture- and stain-resistant and easy to keep in good condition. Also, vinyl hides marred walls because of its weight—a major consideration if you are occupying an old-fashioned apartment where walls are scarred.

All manner of colors and patterns are now on the market, including florals, stripes, trellis and lattice designs, plaids, and modern abstract wall coverings. There are lovely patterns evoking the sea that feature shells, sea flora, seascapes, and the like. The pattern you select will depend on your taste and the overall decorative mood you want to achieve.

Wall coverings with a metallic background are particularly effective in a bathroom. They introduce a sense of spaciousness because of their reflective qualities, plus a hint of glamor and luxury as well. The most popular metallic backgrounds are silver, gold, and copper, with the pattern in another color. However, metallic blues, reds, greens, and yellows are also available.

For a sense of coordination throughout, and to expand the feeling of space, carry the wall covering up onto the ceiling and use it to line the inside of the door. If the wall covering you select has a matching fabric, consider using this to make tieback draperies for the bath. These should be hung at ceiling level and should fall to the floor. However, these should not be used in place of a shower curtain; they are merely decorative. Hang an opaque shower curtain on the shower rod and pull it back behind one of the draperies when not in use.

LACQUER PAINTS

If you prefer to paint your bathroom walls, consider all the newest lacquer paints. These come in a seemingly endless range of colors, from pretty pastels to the more vivid reds, blues, fir greens, and brown. Like metallic wall coverings, they introduce a touch of glamor because of their sheen. Use lacquer on the walls above the tiles, on the ceiling, and on all woodwork to produce a smooth, unbroken look. One color used throughout is more restful and expands space because the eye is not stopped by contrasts. Accent colors can be introduced in linens, accessories, and floor coverings.

STICK-ON PLASTIC TILES

If you want to dress up the plain white tiles in your bathroom, you can use the stick-on plastic tiles now on the market, which are actually like decals. They are lightweight and usually have a transparent background overlaid with a simple design. The tiles are self-adhesive and are simple to put in place. Their transparent background permits the color of the actual wall tile to show through, so that the design on the decal comes into prominence. A variety of colors and designs are available so that you can produce interesting effects. However, a word of warning: Don't cover every tile in the bathroom with decals. Create a random design instead, since this is not so overpowering and much easier to live with.

ACCESSORIES

Whatever the size of the bathroom you are decorating, it does need accessories to give it a finished look. Naturally, what you select depends on your personal taste and the overall effect you want to create.

Consider using wall-hung shelves if you have little or no available counter space. Glass, clear plastic, or Plexiglas shelves are ideal because of their light-as-air look. Bottles of perfume, interesting ornaments, and ceramic or plastic pots for powder and other cosmetic aids can all be displayed on shelves. Such things as tissue holders, toothbrush mugs, wastepaper baskets, and towel holders all add a decorative touch; a custom-designed effect is created when these items are all matched.

Plants thrive in a bathroom because of the dampness. These can be suspended from the ceiling, held in brackets on a wall, or arranged in a corner, depending on the available space. Before buying plants for a bathroom, consider the degree of light, if any, that comes into the room and make sure the types you choose are adapted for survival in this environment.

Although linens are essential in a bathroom, they also come under the heading of accessories. For a totally coordinated feeling, a custom-designed look, and a sense of luxury, select bath linens that are harmonious with your overall color scheme. This is a cinch today, since towels and bath mats come in every conceivable shade. Select linens that match the color of the walls or, alternatively, choose them in a constrasting shade that adds just the right accent color. If you have used a patterned wall covering, you may want to choose linens that pick up one of the colors in the pattern.

How to Treat the Floor

Most apartment bathrooms have a tiled floor. When the latter is in good condition, there is no reason why you cannot leave it as it is. You can then add a touch of comfort by using a large bath mat. If the floor is chipped, scuffed, or in bad condition, you may want to cover it up if you cannot go to the expense of putting down new tiles.

The best product to use in this instance is the latest bathroom carpeting, which can be purchased in most department and carpet stores. It comes in rolls and can be cut to the desired size to fit your bathroom floor. Colors come in a wide range, and most textures are soft and fluffy. The beauty of this type of bathroom carpeting is that it can be pulled up and machine-washed. You might also consider using it even if your floor is in good condition, since it does introduce warmth. Pick a color that fulfills the basic color scheme of the walls and linens.

If you have utilized wall-to-wall carpeting in a bedroom, you can use this same carpeting in an adjoining bathroom to create a smooth, unbroken look between the two rooms. Standard carpeting wears well in a bathroom, although it is usually wise to add a bath mat to give it a little protection.

Vinyl, rubber, and ceramic tiles also take to the bathroom scene with ease. Interesting decorative effects can be created with any of these. Although they are not as warm underfoot as carpeting, they can be dressed up with a bath mat. They are all durable and easy to maintain.

Expanding the Feeling of Space

Counteracting the confined feeling so prevalent in many apartment bathrooms is not quite as difficult as it sounds. The easiest way to do this is by using materials that create a sense of spaciousness through visual illusion.

Color is a handy tool for making space seem larger. As was pointed out earlier, pale and light colors recede, helping to push walls out, and the ceiling upward. White, neutral tones, and pastels are ideal for creating this effect. Avoid vivid or dark colors if your bathroom gives you a claustrophobic feeling, as these tend to advance and make the physical space seem much smaller.

Silver wall coverings and any others that have a light-toned metallic background create an illusion of additional space. This is so because their surfaces reflect light, bouncing it back into the room.

A mirrored surface is obviously the one thing that is unbeatable when it comes to introducing greater spaciousness in a bathroom—or any other room, for that matter. All types of mirrors are available: plain, smoked, antique, or frosted. Mirrored panels can be put on walls throughout the bathroom—even on the ceiling, if you so desire. The effect is one of lightness and airiness, full of shimmering surfaces and reflected images. Like silver wall coverings, mirrors bounce light back into the room. Of course, mirrored panels are quite expensive and must be installed by a professional. On the other hand, you can purchase mirrored tiles that can be affixed with a strong adhesive. They do help to produce a similar ambience and are much less costly. However, they, too, should be installed by a professional since they can be tricky to handle.

Discovering Extra Storage Space

When space is at a premium in a bathroom, storage areas often suffer. However, there are ways to add extra storage space through a bit of ingenuity.

A sink with ugly exposed pipes looks unattractive; also, the space underneath it is basically wasted. For as little as one hundred dollars you can buy a ready-made vanity that fits around the sink and can be easily installed by a carpenter. The vanity adds a bit of extra counter space around the top of the washbasin. Doors in its base create a cupboard out of the floor space underneath, which can be used to house toilet articles, cleaning products, and materials.

Make use of the inside of the bathroom door by hanging a medicine cabinet on it. All manner of items can be stored on the shelves, freeing the counter space they have been occupying for other things.

One of the newest and most unique shower curtains now on the market contains stitched-on pockets to hold such things as shampoo, conditioner, and a variety of other items used in the bath. This, too, is a storage item that is practical and inexpensive.

Many manufacturers are now producing scaled-down chests and sets of shelves that fit neatly into the corner of a bathroom. Fashioned of plastic and available in stunning decorator colors, they are perfect for storing linens, toilet articles, and the like. The top provides a bit of extra counter space for displaying accessories or a plant.

Lighting the Bathroom

Like a kitchen, a bathroom requires good lighting, especially if there is no window or other source of natural daylight. Here are a few pointers.

Avoid lighting products that produce a harsh effect, create glare, and distort color. Fluorescent strip lighting tends to do the latter.

Select lighting fixtures that give out clear, bright light and do not produce shadowy areas within the space.

Be certain you have good lighting above all mirrors.

Add a ceiling light for overall illumination if the room is large.

Supplementary lighting should be included if you have vanity and dressing areas.

Remember that dark colors absorb more light than pale tones. If the color scheme of your bathroom is in deep or vivid shades, use strong bulbs or strip lighting to obtain the best results.

Planning efficient lighting for the bathroom is not that difficult once you are aware of the aforementioned points. There are a range of new products to choose from, all of which can help you to solve the majority of lighting problems encountered while decorating the average apartment bathroom.

OVERLEAF A kitchen scheme can start with any one of several elements, including floors, walls, cabinets, or counters. The decorating scheme for this kitchen began with the red marble floor—which was already in place—to which designer *Michael Jackson* matched cabinets and wall covering. His aim, however, was more than just designing an attractive kitchen. It was to create a pleasant and convenient environment, through cosmetic rather than structural remodeling, for a client who enjoys entertaining but not cooking. The emphasis was on easy maintenance as well. Many apartment dwellers are faced with a similar challenge, namely, how to adapt to specific needs a kitchen that is functional and sufficiently spacious but lacking in interest. Appliances were considered first. Outdated equipment was replaced but not shifted around. The ceiling was lowered to improve the proportions of what was a long, narrow room and make it appear wider. Rather than replacing cabinets, Jackson had them painted Chinese red with a lacquer finish. The color is warm and easy to live with. The wall covering, which was custom-colored to match, is a vinyl with Chinese hieroglyphics in jade green (almost black) on a red patent ground. The pagoda red blind, chosen later, exactly matches cabinets and wall covering. When closed it makes the kitchen look cozy. While open it reveals a view of the Manhattan skyline and lets in sunshine to encourage plant growth. Though the flooring is marble, it could as easily be vinyl, which likewise requires minimal maintenance. Counters and backsplash are of high-pressure laminate in simulated butcher block—another easy-care element—as is the thin-slatted aluminum blind.

The blind, incidentally, features a new valance that comes with it. The latter consists of two color-matched slats that you attach to the head rail to bridge the narrow space between the head and top slat. The valance adds a finishing touch to the blind, which is the simplest and most effective of today's window treatments. It is neither a dust catcher nor a space snatcher. It can be adjusted easily by means of a translucent wand and can be raised or lowered with a thin, almost invisible cord.

Zesta
club

This kitchen in an old-fashioned apartment was spacious, but it was badly planned as far as the positioning of equipment and alignment of cabinets was concerned. Also, these were all old and outdated. New equipment was installed and was aligned along the wall next to the new sink (not visible). The latter is housed in a long counter with base storage underneath and laminated work surfaces. A metal rack for utensils was placed above the sink, along with a clock. A spare wall at one end of the kitchen was filled with floor-to-ceiling cabinets, with a central space left free for another work counter. (This counter also doubles as a desk when required.) Centralization of all cabinets makes for real efficiency. White paint gives the whole room a fresh, airy look, while the plaid carpet underfoot adds a dash of rich green, red, and black. This carpet, made of nylon, is hard-wearing for this heavy traffic area. Because of the size of the kitchen it was possible to include a small dining table and bentwood chairs. The total revamping operation, done on a medium budget, gave the kitchen a new, modern atmosphere and made possible greater efficiency.

A well-organized work area was created in this medium-sized kitchen, with maximum use being made of the walls to save floor space. Two butcher block tables that form an L-shape provide counter space for working and eating. They are practical and sturdy and just a few steps away from the equipment and sink on the opposite wall (not visible). Hooks under one of the tables hold pans, while a large piece of pegboard efficiently holds all manner of utensils, placing them within easy reach for food preparation. Shelves on the adjoining walls and above the window hold cookbooks, extra utensils, and pottery. To revamp an old-fashioned window, cafe curtains were hung, topped by a window shade. The old scuffed floor was treated to a brightly colored practical kitchen carpet made of 100 percent nylon, which is hard-wearing and easy to maintain since spots and spills can be wiped up quickly. To complete this inexpensive revamping job, the walls were painted a soft green accented by white woodwork.

This tiny kitchen was so confined that it seemed to defy decoration. But interior designer *Charlotte Finn,* A.S.I.D., gave it good looks and greater efficiency through clever planning and designing. She took advantage of a little space in the window area and built a curved counter that narrows at one end near the sink. It provides extra work space and doubles as a snack counter as well; it is serviced by the small wicker stool that tucks neatly underneath. Cabinet space was provided along the wall above the sink and in the window area, where a set of open shelves are used to display attractive accessories. An extra cupboard was included under the work counter at the right. All cupboards have Plexiglas handles and are painted a bright Siamese pink. White painted walls and counter tops cool the hot color, as does the white window shade trimmed with pink cutouts; the latter were fashioned from the wallpaper left over from the ceiling treatment. Completing the revamping job is a white vinyl tile floor. All surfaces are maintenance-free and can be wiped clean in a jiffy.

OVERLEAF Interior designer *Angelo Donghia,* A.S.I.D., gave a brand-new look to this kitchen through the use of the latest materials and the newest equipment. He gutted the old-fashioned kitchen and started from scratch, installing such things as double-wall ovens, range, sink, and dishwasher—all made of stainless steel. Stainless steel counter tops and cabinets ranged around the room enhance the reflective, shiny look and help to open up space considerably. Once the equipment was installed, the designer covered the remaining wall areas with black and white ceramic tiles. These were also used for the floor in a smaller pattern for a change of pace that was still within the basic color scheme. Underscoring this color combination is the woodwork, which was painted dark gray. An old-fashioned window was treated to a silver-colored aluminum blind. It is balanced on either side by stained-glass windows, which the designer decided to leave intact for decorative purposes. This revamping effort proves what an excellent job can be done with an old-fashioned kitchen in a turn-of-the-century apartment building.

Although this kitchen was spacious and modern, it was somewhat sterile in appearance. Green and white checked vinyl paper and a coordinate design overlaid with tomatoes was used throughout to introduce a sense of color, pattern, and warmth. The checked paper was repeated on all the cabinets on either side of the window and underneath the sink and range area. It was also carried up onto the ceiling for a real sense of coordination. The tomato-patterned coordinate design was run along the area just below the ceiling and then carried over onto the side wall. Here a built-in shelf adjoining the work surface under the window acts as a snack counter, which is serviced by two wood and cane chairs. The entire counter space is lined with a plastic laminate that simulates butcher block wood and is practical and hard-wearing. The floor was treated to white vinyl tiles interspersed with bands of green. A green hood was utilized over the range. Such things as the matchstick blind, wooden clock, and the freestanding butcher block chopping table add finishing touches.

Herbal
tea
herbs
for the kitchen

In its original state this bathroom was typical of those found in an old-fashioned apartment. Small in size, the walls were cut up with white tiles and there was an unattractive overhead beam near the window. The floor was chipped and in poor condition. Interior designer *Virginia Frankel,* A.S.I.D., began her revamping by using a prettily colored patchwork wall covering on the walls and ceiling and along the beam. The candy-colored wall covering helped to lighten the somewhat confined room and introduced a cheery mood. A pink bathroom carpet was put down on the floor and matching pink covers for toilet tank and seat were used to create a coordinated look. Bath mat and towels are of the same shade, which repeats the dominant pink in the green, yellow, and blue wall covering. Pieces of the latter were used to cover the cupboard built around the sink, which the designer added to hide ugly pipes. It is made of plywood and is easy for a carpenter to install. To partially hide an unattractive window the designer put up brass brackets and glass shelves; a variety of plants are displayed here. More plants are hung from the ceiling and the beam. Decorative accessories add finishing touches.

Even the tiniest of bathrooms can be given a handsome and highly decorative look through a little clever decorating. The secret of this room's success is the bandanna-patterned wall covering and coordinated fabric used lavishly throughout. The cool mingling of greens and white and the squared-off pattern help to open up the room and make it seem larger. The vinyl was carried up onto the ceiling and above the tiles in the bath area. Tieback curtains with frilled edges were hung on a pole at ceiling level; they help to give a grand look to the little room. The floor (not visible) was treated to a green bathroom carpet for added color harmony and luxury underfoot. A handsome antique chandelier, old-fashioned prints, and other accessories help to underscore the mood of elegance that was achieved here.

As was previously pointed out, rejuvenating a bathroom need not be an expensive project involving ripping out and replacing. Of course, it is nice to do this if you have antiquated fixtures and a sizable budget to buy new ones, but you can also do a lot by being creative. Start with a pretty wall covering and use it not only on walls but also on cupboard doors and the front of a vanity, as shown here. The latter was built to camouflage plumbing and to introduce a lovely, sleek look. Select a color from the wall covering as the tone for painting woodwork and other trim. Here designer *Shirley Regendahl* chose the bright blue of the wall covering's pink, green, and blue print on a white ground. She used this color to edge doors and shelves, as well as on the molding added for decorative trim. White rubber flooring was put down. Once the basic surfaces were decorated, the designer added decorative interest in the form of a unique shell mirror, an old print, a tiny wooden chest, together with other decorative accessories made of porcelain and melamine.

A lot can be achieved with very little money, as is illustrated here in this small bathroom, where space was really at a premium. Because the owner of the apartment was working on a limited budget, ingenuity was of prime importance. The side wall was covered with a green and white checked wall covering; the bright green was repeated in the toilet seat cover and bath mat. White plastic towel holders and a white circular mirror were mounted on the side wall. The towels repeat the green and white used throughout. The decorative focal point of the little bath is the plastic shower curtain. This charming design features a zebra amid a profusion of green and yellow flowers. The zebra is, of course, striped in black and white.

harmonious with more rustic styles, such as Early American. However, it can be sometimes used most effectively with modern designs. On the other hand, a more coarse texture, such as a nubby tweed or cotton, works well with country-style furnishings. Belgian linen, cotton, cotton-velvet, velvet, wool, felt, and simulated suede or leather all help to beautify and dramatize walls. Consider all of these materials before making your final choice.

Vinyl and wallpaper can be applied in unusual ways to create interesting effects. They can be hung in panels on the walls, carried up onto the ceiling, and used to line the insides of doors. You can be even more inventive with fabrics. They, too, can be hung in panels, shirred to the walls, and stretched across ceilings, depending on the overall decorative mood you want to produce.

Interior designer *Joan Blutter*, F.A.S.I.D., recommends tenting a room with fabric or sheets to introduce dramatic, highly decorative overtones and a custom-designed look. She also points out that the fabric camouflages marred walls and ceilings—a major consideration, particularly if you live in an old apartment with poor wall surfaces.

To tent a room correctly, begin by attaching narrow strips of wood all around the walls at ceiling and floor level. The fabric or sheets should be cut to the desired length, hemmed, and then shirred. These individual panels of fabric are then stapled to the wood strips at top and bottom. This designer prefers stapling, as the staples are easy to pull out when the fabric needs to be taken down and laundered. However, this is usually not necessary more than once a year, as the fabric can be kept dust-free through vacuuming. Incidentally, when fabric is shirred onto the wall the staples are usually not visible. If they are, they can be covered by using decorative braid as a border at ceiling and floor level. Lengths of fabric intended to cover the ceiling are measured, cut, hemmed, and shirred in the same way; they are then stretched across the ceiling tautly to create the right effect. Joan likes to use matching fabric at the windows and on the bed for a totally coordinated effect.

PANELING

A handsome look can be produced in a room through the use of wood paneling or decorator paneling that simulates wood. The latter comes in wood tones as well as bright, solid colors.

Most paneling is precut today, which makes it relatively easy to put up yourself with the aid of a special adhesive that is sold with it. Almost all brands of paneling come in a variety of designs that blend with both period and modern furniture. Paneling creates a lovely warm, mellow backdrop for furniture, adds architectural interest to the walls, and is easy to maintain. Apart from these qualities, paneling is durable, hard-wearing, and helps to soundproof a room as well as insulate it.

Select your paneling carefully, paying attention to the color of the wood. Remember, dark wood tones tend to advance, thereby reducing a room's spaciousness through visual illusion. Light wood tones tend to recede and thus help to make the same space look much larger.

Highlighting the Floor

A unique floor treatment helps to dramatize a room. There are many products that help you to create stunning effects. Of course, the type you select must be in keeping with the decorative scheme and should also be practical from every point of view.

Stenciled floors are becoming popular again. They are very pretty in most rooms, but especially in bedrooms, living rooms, nurseries, or children's rooms. Stenciling kits are available at art stores and are not all that costly. Complete instructions come with the kits to aid you in creating interesting patterns and designs. A wood floor must be cleaned and refinished before the pattern is stenciled on it. Some interior designers like to paint the floor a light color before stenciling. Once the pattern is in place and has dried, the floor should be treated with several coats of polyurethane to seal and protect it from scuffing.

Vinyl tiles can be utilized to create striking effects. For instance, a tile of one color can be used on most of the floor; then a border and central motif can be created with tiles of a contrasting color or colors. The finished result resembles an area rug. Or tiles of two different colors, perhaps black and white, can be used to introduce a checkerboard surface underfoot. The color combinations for this type of treatment are endless: black and red; blue and green; yellow and white; and blue and white. Stripes, abstract designs, and custom-designed effects can be produced through an imaginative use of tiles in different colors.

Carpet tiles are now available at moderate cost. They can be arranged to create the same effect as vinyl tiles. Moveover, they are ideal for people on a budget since they are a do-it-yourself product; the tiles come with a self-adhesive backing and are simply stuck to the floor.

Area rugs of modern design are highly decorative, helping to introduce color, pattern, and textural interest underfoot. Many of these rugs are so beautifully designed that they resemble wall hangings. They are perfect for highlighting a wood floor and pinpointing a furniture arrangement.

Painted floors are currently in vogue. Many leading interior designers are featuring them in their latest settings. The most popular colors are white or sand. The wood floor is cleaned, sanded down to its natural light color, and then refinished. It is then painted with several coats of floor paint and left to dry. Polyurethane is then used to seal and protect it. A painted floor in a light color helps to expand the feeling of space in a room and serves as a cool backdrop for area rugs of both modern and traditional design. Of course, if you want to be daring you can paint the floor a vibrant color, such as bright red or dark blue, and then highlight it with pale area rugs.

Dramatic Lighting

As was pointed out earlier, lighting helps to introduce a particular mood into a room. Certain fixtures and techniques definitely create a dramatic effect. If you want to use lighting to this end, bear in mind that the room must be comfortably illuminated—neither too harsh nor too dark. So plan your dramatic effects carefully so that you can live with them around the clock.

Track lighting installed on the ceiling is ideal for a room where lots of art is displayed on the walls. The track lighting fixtures swivel in any direction and can be angled to focus attention on paintings or a piece of sculpture in another part of the room. Track lighting works well in rooms of contemporary or eclectic design.

Spot lighting helps to highlight accessories on shelves, a single piece of sculpture on a pedestal, and plants. Interesting effects of shadow and light can be introduced if you place the spots in strategic areas of the room, with the direction of the light angled toward the object.

Cornice and valance lighting is similar to cove lighting and is used to focus attention on windows and window treatments. The lighting should be placed behind a valance or cornice to throw light upward for ceiling reflection and downward for direct window or drapery illumination. The source of the light must be hidden from view. The effect is highly dramatic, enhancing decorative themes in modern and traditional rooms.

Furniture lighting can be used to focus attention on various decorative objects. Bookshelves, wall niches, and shelves and cabinets can be lighted by incandescent or fluorescent lamps installed in hidden locations adjoining, or in various parts of the framework of, the furniture. These lights are usually directed toward the back of the shelving to illuminate particular objects and accessories.

Bulbs of different colors create a variety of moods in any room. This is a very inexpensive way of introducing a dramatic touch. For instance, pink, red, aqua, and yellow bulbs produce lovely decorative effects. A pink bulb diffuses a soft, warm light that picks up the reds, oranges, or other warm colors in a decorative scheme. The mood is generally flattering to people as well as to the room.

An aqua bulb is used to cool an intense or hot color scheme. It accentuates the blues in a room and makes them seem slightly more intense for a really dramatic look. A yellow bulb creates a sunny effect and also enriches all the yellows and sand tones in a scheme. A red bulb produces a rosy glow and must be used carefully to avoid an intensely hot effect.

How to Create Added Drama

You can introduce added drama into the standard room through the utilization of other elements and products. Here is a basic checklist.

1. Mirrors work magic in a room of any size and design. They help to expand the feeling of space and can be used to highlight a particular area or create a shimmering reflective backdrop for furniture. When used over a large area, they

can be highly dramatic, especially when they reflect interesting images or a scenic view through large windows. Lighting fixtures or candles placed close to a mirror underscore its shimmering effect and can be most eye-catching.

2. Wall murals and super-graphics help to give walls a new dimension, often creating a three-dimensional quality that is quite unique. Super-graphics are usually hand-painted; they should be done by a professional to be really successful. They are generally positioned in the middle of a wall so that they are clearly visible, make the correct decorative impact, and do not compete with furniture placed against the wall. The same rules apply to murals. Scenic and mural wallpapers are readily available today and come in charming designs. They help to create the same effect as hand-painted murals and super-graphics, yet are easy to hang yourself and don't cost as much.

3. Color can be utilized to make a dramatic statement in a room. An unusual combination of colors used for an overall scheme is not only decorative but invokes a given mood and also says something about you and your tastes. Some unusual color combinations are purple accented with pink and cooled by white; brown flashed with mint green and yellow; blue highlighted by red and toned down with white; red accented with dark green; fir green sparked by pale blue or highlighted with white; and midnight blue charged with yellow touches.

A single color used throughout a room can also be highly dramatic. White used for everything and enlivened with accent colors for accessories is most luxurious-looking; it creates a spacious and restful mood. An all-red room is striking, warm, and intimate. However, this is a hard color to live with over a long period, so be sure you won't tire of it before you start decorating.

4. Unique accessories will add flair and character to a bland room. They must be displayed with imagination to make the greatest impact and, as was pointed out earlier, they should be well illuminated for maximum visual pleasure. A single piece of sculpture on a pedestal is most effective in front of a window. A large piece of sculpture placed on the floor next to an arrangement of plants makes a strong decorative statement. Alternatively, you can arrange collections of other objects to produce a striking effect. African art, native handicrafts, American Indian crafts, and similar items picked up while traveling or collected over the years will help to give a room added visual excitement.

There are many ways to dramatize a bland room. The ideas, products, and techniques you select will depend on your taste. But always remember that the end result should be harmonious and comfortable, an environment you will enjoy occupying.

Interior designer *Peg Walker* thought big when decorating a small dining room by leaning heavily on two do-it-yourself techniques that add elegance, color, and drama. Sunlit yellow blinds made of shade cloth sheathe the windows. This up-to-the-minute treatment isn't as expensive as it appears. The component parts were specially cut to size, with hardware that is easy to assemble. Underfoot, a handsome area rug combines a wine center with a lush citron shag border. This custom look is achieved by means of another new technique with "ready-mades" that won't break the bank. The shag and velvet plush were ordered individually and joined with carpet seaming tape. Imaginative ideas spark the rest of the decor as well. A narrow shelf covered in plastic laminate was run across the window to play a sideboard role. The beams to which it is attached have been camouflaged by mirrored sides and facings painted a rich, deep wine that matches the rug. The glass-topped table's see-through qualities help to maintain the illusion of space. Walnut plantation chairs add a curvaceous note—repeated in a stunning yellow and wine abstract by Charles Hix. Truly individual in flavor, this charming "put together" room boasts still another unseen advantage. The vinyl-coated shade cloth and the rug both yield quickly to the swoosh of a damp cloth—an important plus anywhere, particularly in a dining room.

OVERLEAF This living room in an apartment designed by *Michael Sherman* takes on a wonderful, exciting character through the application of imaginative techniques that give it drama and decorative impact. Ordinary double-hung windows are treated to textured vertical blinds; ceiling to floor slats control light. Mirrored lambrequins surrounding the blinds highlight the area and reflect the various elements in the room. This window treatment opens up space considerably while adding sophistication. Balancing the uniquely treated window wall is the adjacent wall, covered in a plum and white wall covering decorated in a light, airy plaid pattern. This makes a good backdrop for the two plum-colored sofas deftly placed in an L-shape around a white Lucite coffee table. Unfinished campaign chests were covered with silver lizard-type vinyl; the drawers were outlined with chrome nailheads and then finished with stainless steel pulls. The burgundy and orange colors in the paintings and in the lavish collection of needlepoint cushions are dashing accents, while other accessories, such as the sculpture and ceramic items, also make definitive statements. The finished result is a previously bland room transformed into one that is all shimmer and sheen, underscored by a burgundy shag rug.

BEFORE This large, high-ceilinged room in a vintage apartment still shows traces of its former glory despite the exposed radiator, pipe, peeling paint, and plaster. A deeply recessed window has folding shutters that are slightly warped and no longer function too well. AFTER Revamped, the garden-fresh room, decorated around a delightful carpet, takes all of its colors and motifs from the print on the floor. A stenciled trellis motif from the carpet decorates the blue window shade as well as the matching do-it-yourself screen covered with extra shade cloth. The latter makes an easy and effective camouflage for the exposed radiator and pipe. The same Bristol blue color from the carpet is used to outline the window's deep recess, contrasting effectively with the cream tone on the walls, also taken from the carpet. Even the octagonal shade pull, cut from plywood, is painted cream to match. The wall-to-wall carpeting continues up the face of a two-tiered plant stand that fits the window's triangular shape. Another do-it-yourself idea is the round table skirted in a spatter-dash print that combines all of the same soft-focus blues, greens, and creamy tones. Designed by *Ann Heller,* the sunny, plant-filled room blends drama and practicality. The vinyl-coated shade cloth can be sponged clean, as can the wicker chaise. The carpet combines rugged, soil-resistant qualities with permanent antistatic control to eliminate annoying electric shocks.

Artist Bobjack Callejo produced the striking wrap-around graphic that encircles this unusual den created by *Ann Heller* together with *Jane Cohler Ross*. The broad red line, edged with narrow black wood stripping to create a three-dimensional effect, zigzags across the walls, ceiling, and perpendicularly down white room-darkening window shades. The treatment brings drama and interest to an otherwise bland room. The audaciously conceived den offers round-the-clock service. In front of one window a handsome, sturdy white vinyl convertible sofa joins forces with a pair of red-and-chrome scoop chairs positioned around a coffee table. On one side of the convertible a compartmentalized Plexiglas end table constructed by the owners adds multifaceted, transparent storage. On the other side a black standing lamp sports adjustable chrome "light-up-anywhere" spots. Close at hand are pillows in appropriately bright colors; they lie in wait to make floor games cozier for kids. Across the room a Plexiglas bridge table has been set up for cards or dining. Even the acrylic-painted window shades, so integral a part of the dramatic background, do double duty, contributing privacy and "blackout" service when guests sleep over.

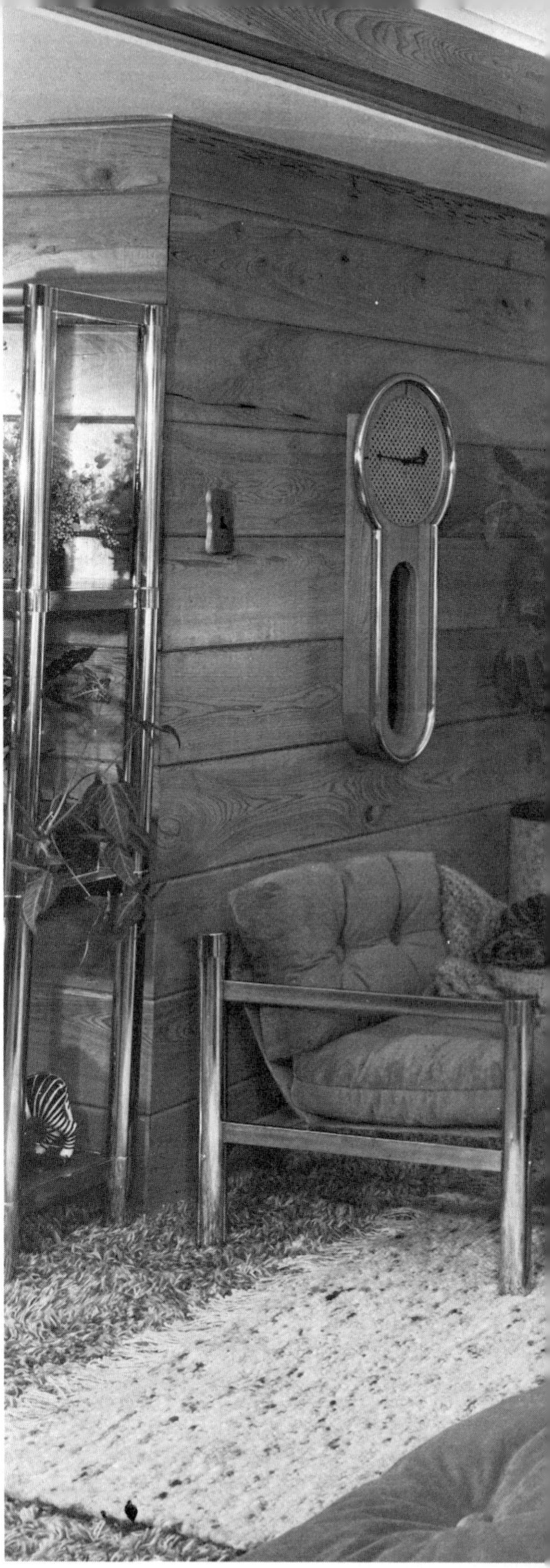

Paneling sets the stage and warms the environment of a room totally devoid of any architectural interest. Instead of installing the paneling in the usual vertical pattern, pecky cypress paneling was installed horizontally. This visually enlarged the room and added a new dimension of character to the space. Intent on a casual life-style, the owner selected chrome-framed furniture to provide textural contrast and easy care. Chrome étagères display art objects and plants, while the wood theme is repeated in the tabletops, which have a stained oak banding and a tempered-glass center. As can readily be seen, texture plays an important part in the success of this living room, which features deep rust and camel cotton velvet upholstery, a wicker chest, a contemporary wall clock in wood and chrome, and wool carpeting in beiges and browns. Furniture was selected with an eye toward the budget. In fact, the furniture was of the ready-to-assemble type and therefore offered substantial savings. It is engineered to provide durability and long wear.

The dining room in a condominium was revamped by *Charles Lewin*, A.S.I.D. His eclectic mix-and-match approach is refreshing and introduces decorative overtones. Nineteenth-century romanticism serves as a starting point in his decorating scheme, which calls for an elegant blending of styles and periods. The room takes on a fresh mood through the use of wall coverings and related fabrics, add-on architecture, and well-chosen furniture. A charming geometric print, obviously appropriate for cozy, intimate gatherings, complements the oversized botanical print used in the adjoining living room (also visible). The neutral schemes in both rooms, composed of beiges, whites and blues, create a visual flow from one room to the other, again enhancing the feeling of spaciousness. Add-on architecture, including molding and ceiling beams, punctuates the fabric-covered walls and ceiling, providing extra definition and interest. The contemporary glass dining table with tortoiseshell legs, the Early American hutch, and the bamboo-turned wood dining chairs were all chosen for their style and timeless appeal. Antique chandelier, plants, and wall prints echo the country mood first established in the living room and successfully repeated here.

OVERLEAF A small run-of-the-mill condominium was transformed into a charming and gracious environment by interior designer *Charles Lewin*, A.S.I.D., who selected appropriate wall coverings and related fabrics to accomplish this. He turned to nineteenth-century romanticism for the overall effect. This called for an elegant blending of styles and periods, enriched by interesting architectural details and a generous use of pattern. For the living room he selected a quaint botanical print that gives the room a country look and provides warmth and decorative flair. The oversized pattern helps to open up the room's limited dimensions and create a fresh, airy ambience. The cold, concrete slab floor was then covered with oak finished in a handsome parquet pattern. Although relatively expensive, the cost of installing a wood floor is a wise investment. It is the epitome of elegance, provides marvelous insulation, is easy to maintain, and never has to be replaced. To create decorative and architectural interest, beams were run up the walls and across the ceiling to underscore the authentic country charm; they also help focus attention on the pattern. Full-length mirrors flanking the fireplace wall seem to double the room's dimensions. The designer truly personalized the room by mixing and matching accessories. The English wing chair, the Moroccan rug, the Chinese sculpture—all have great style and timeless appeal. A profusion of flowers and plants act as sources of color, pattern, texture, and elegance in a room of new dimensions.

PRECEDING PAGES A city apartment bedroom can take on a gracious country air through the use of accessories, color, and add-on architecture. Simulated curved wood beams can be installed easily. In this bedroom they were arranged to provide a frame for an old brass headboard. They continue around the room and thus unify the whole area. Stained wooden shutters at the window help to underscore the country cottage feeling so predominant here. A baker's rack bought at a secondhand store lends charm and functions as a display for plants and antique cachepots. A floral bed ensemble in deep, muted colors set against a beige background is the coloristic focal point; it is accentuated by the deep rose-colored wall. At the foot of the bed a Pennsylvania Dutch blanket chest stores nonseasonal clothes; there is additional storage space beneath the skirted round bedside table. Seating is provided through the inclusion of a refinished ladder-back rocking chair that again underscores the rustic flavor. Beige wall-to-wall carpeting adds comfort and luxury underfoot and serves as a neutral background for the color scheme of walls and bed ensemble, as well as the dark wood tones.

OPPOSITE There are several ways to revitalize a mundane room. One of the simplest is to add architectural elements and utilize a sparkling color scheme. In this rather uninteresting room in a remodeled brownstone apartment, a favorite American color scheme of red, white, and blue was used throughout to create a lively and cheerful atmosphere. White wood paneling was installed to cover cracked and bumpy walls, while rustic brown beams were interspersed every four feet. This treatment not only gave additional architectural dimension to the space but also covered the butt seams in the paneling. A flag blue area rug sits atop white brick-patterned vinyl flooring, while a red and blue plaid fabric was used for the bedspread and cafe curtains at the oddly proportioned window. In fact, a gable-type effect was created through the special installation over the window. A dark blue wing chair, plus reproductions of Early American furniture, provide a definite rustic country setting in the heart of a big city. With the proper tools and equipment, this can be a weekend do-it-yourself project for the handy Sunday carpenter. A brass headboard, jug-base lamp with linen lampshade, pewter accessories, and greenery further enhance this peaceful and restful bedroom, which also has decorative impact.

OVERLEAF Fabric is the catalyst in this high-rise bedroom designed for comfort, good looks, and great eye appeal. A handsome four-poster is the very center and focal point of this unique setting, which might just as well be in the country rather than a city apartment. Curved wooden bedposts are balanced by the headboard, which acts as a display background for botanical prints that have been applied in decoupage fashion to wooden plaques. A traditional, multicolored patchwork quilt —made by the owner with loving and painstaking attention to detail—adds additional color and pattern. A black and white leaf-patterned fabric lined with black and white tattersall sheeting makes for an unusual combination to curtain the bed. The tattersall sheeting is also used to cover the canopy of the bed as well as the comfortable easy chair. Fabric-covered pillows in a variety of prints are strewn on bed and chair to introduce color and decorative accents. Plain white sheeting is utilized for the curtains, while the overdrapes consist of the same black and white leaf pattern. Somewhat different, but definitively dramatic, is the black fabric used to upholster the back wall. Wall upholstery is especially utilitarian, since it insulates as well as deadens sound. Beige embossed carpeting echoes the warmth and character of the overall decor. Photographs are displayed prominently to provide charm and dramatic emphasis in this revamped bedroom.

DEB
DEB
DEB

An enchanting country-garden mood is introduced by this scenic-design wall covering. It works wonders for a little play area located in a rather small country-style living room in a high-rise apartment short on architectural features. The design of this wall covering gives the illusion of space and creates windows where there are none. Colors such as green, yellow, blue, and white with lovely rose-red accents are utilized in the pattern and suggest springtime the year round. A vivid grass green carpet used throughout the living room underscores and controls the overall scene. Backgammon, a favorite family game, is especially enjoyable when played at the mahogany backgammon table bought at a country auction. Refinishing of the table was done at leisure during long weekends. Another "find" was an old trunk that was covered in a coordinated floral wall covering and accented with dark brown hardware. It helps to underscore the three-dimensional effect created by the trompe l'oeil pattern.

Built-in units can be utilized to create architectural interest in a room without any, as illustrated here. Two floor-to-ceiling cabinets containing base storage areas and bookshelves were built at either end of a wall. They were given definition with wall covering and add-on molding painted blue to match the broad stripe in the pattern. To create a sense of unity throughout, molding was carried around the room at ceiling and floor level; it was also repeated around the walls for a chair-rail effect. This is further emphasized through the use of striped wall covering below the floral print. Note how the units create an alcove, a cozy spot for the "sofa," which is actually composed of three chairs aligned next to each other. The chairs, which have sled bases of chrome-finished steel, promote a forties feeling in this multipurpose room. Moderately priced, the chairs are held together by a hidden locking device in the base and can be quickly assembled at home. Rust velvet on the chairs picks up the rust in the striped wall covering, while beige wall-to-wall carpeting in a man-made fiber serves as the unifying factor. The dual-purpose units are practical. They can be used to display books and accessories or to hold records, magazines, and the like. At the same time, they add those extra dimensional qualities a bland room needs.

A country look can be achieved in an old-fashioned dining room with the aid of some clever do-it-yourself ideas. A hutch-style corner cabinet was built into one corner of the kitchen to provide both display and storage space. In order to facilitate construction, the design was drawn on a four-foot-by-four-foot plywood panel and cut out by the local lumberyard. Doors and shelves were also precut to specifications and finally assembled on site. A traditional red, white, and blue small-scaled patterned wall covering is used from the ceiling to the top of the chair rail, which was created with white two-inch carved add-on molding. Red paint was utilized underneath the chair rail for a vivid color accent. White ladder-back chairs, stenciled in the same design motif as the wall covering, can be pulled over to the dining table (not visible) for meals. Red and white striped ticking covers the seat cushions and is repeated in the cafe curtains on the opposite wall (not visible). The plank wood floor was painted white, showing off the blue and white geometric sisal rug to great advantage. The floor was treated to several coats of polyurethane to seal and protect it from scuff marks or other damage. Note how the use of fabric, paint, and add-on architectural elements bring decorative interest and a new look to an ordinary little room.

OVERLEAF Custom-designed modular furniture transformed this average studio apartment into a smashing living-dining-sleeping room and also added dramatic impact to bland architecture. All the furniture was scaled to the dimensions inherent in most city apartments and can be used in rooms of all sizes. Compact and compartmentalized living quarters are created through placement of the furniture. The white vinyl sofas are arranged in an L-shape for intimate entertaining. They can be converted into beds at night, providing sleeping facilities for one or two. Surrounding the sofas are blazing red laminated bookshelves, bureaus, and cabinets for displaying books, accessories, and plants; they can also be used for storing clothes. On one wall is a floor-to-ceiling closet, adjacent to a matching floor-to-ceiling bar unit. The latter provides space for bar supplies, dining utensils, and linens. The wall to the left is mirrored, thus enlarging and expanding the feeling of space by means of visual illusion. A narrow-slatted metallic blind controls light around the clock and provides room-darkening qualities at night. White modular lamps introduce warm, glowing illumination and provide a sharp contrast with the all-red shell. The use of red throughout—for the shell, modular pieces, and carpeting—also helps to enlarge the space considerably.

MODERN MOTHERHOOD
BRIDGE CONVENTIONS
THE WORLD SO FAIR
SHELLEY'S DREAM WOMEN
MARGARET CROMPTON
The Making of a
Counter Culture

6 Ways to Give an Entrance Focus

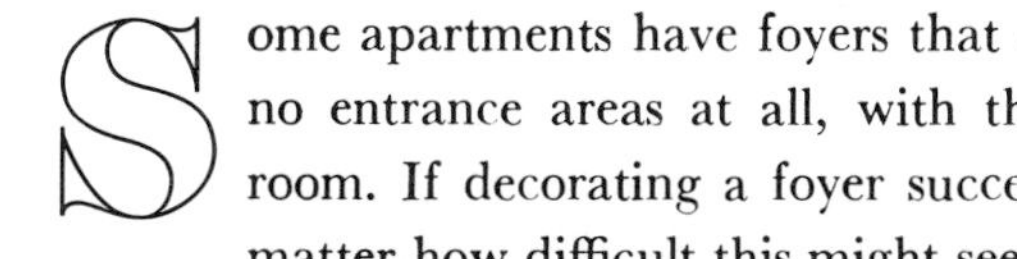

Some apartments have foyers that are small and oddly shaped, while others have no entrance areas at all, with the front door opening directly into the living room. If decorating a foyer successfully is your problem, don't be dismayed no matter how difficult this might seem.

There are many ways to give an entrance a bit of focus so that it says "welcome" to all those entering your home. It can also be a proper introduction to your personal decorating tastes as displayed throughout the rest of the apartment.

Tips for a Small, Boxlike Foyer

A small, boxlike foyer is the one found in most apartments, especially those in modern high-rise buildings. Since this type of foyer is generally perfectly square, lack of space rather than an awkward shape is the main problem. The degree of space will dictate your decorating scheme. There are only two possibilities: You can either make it look larger through a few visual tricks and a clever choice of furnishings or you can turn it into a warm, cozy little box.

Expand the size of the foyer through skillful decorating. Make a basic plan for the shell and execute this first. When this decorating task has been completed, you will get a better picture of the foyer so that you can decide what kind and how much furniture you should include. Here are some suggestions about products for the shell.

Color is one of your best and least expensive decorating tools. Light and pastel-colored paints help to push walls out and make the ceiling appear higher. Select white, sand, cement, banana, primrose, apple, sky blue, or any pastel color you fancy and use it on the walls and ceiling. Carry it over onto all woodwork, the front door, and any closet doors. This flow of unbroken color creates a sense of extra space because the eye is not stopped by contrasts. Consider using lacquer paint, since its shiny surface is reflective and helps to bounce light back into the area. Pale and pastel colors make a nice background for pictures, prints, graphics, ceramic plates, plaques, and other wall accessories—all of which add decorative overtones.

Metallic wall coverings work well in a small foyer, helping to open up the area visually. Both contemporary and traditional patterns are available, as are solid-color metallics that sheathe the walls in silver, gold, copper, and other tones. As with paint, carry the metallic wall covering onto the ceiling and use it on the inside of the front door. If there are any closets in the foyer, cover them with the same wall covering for a smooth look. Incidentally, these metallics make a handsome background for a large mirror, works of art, and accessories.

Certain fabrics help to introduce a spacious feeling. Solid-color fabrics are best, preferably those with a strong texture, such as linen, nubby cotton, or tweed. Stay with light or natural colors that tend to recede. Carry the fabric onto the ceiling and use it on all doors. Matching paint should be used on any other woodwork, such as door trims, molding, and baseboards. Fabrics should be stapled into position and the staples hidden with braid trim used as a border at floor and ceiling level. Textured fabrics, silk, and grass cloth all make a handsome backdrop for artworks, a large mirror, or shelves displaying accessories.

A mirrored surface is the best space expander. Some eye-catching effects can be created in a small foyer. You can cover one wall and seemingly double the size of the space. If you cover two facing walls, the space seems endless. Cover all the walls, doors, and ceiling and you create a glittering mirrored box that fills the area with reflected light. Consider plain, smoked, or antique mirrored surfaces and either utilize the large panels available or, if budget is a major problem, look at the mirrored tiles on the market. A mirrored wall (or walls) serves as a shimmering background for such accessories as plants, objects grouped on a glass or Plexiglas table, or sculpture resting on Plexiglas pedestals.

Floor coverings are important, since the right one will help to visually stretch space underfoot. A bare wood or vinyl tile floor always looks larger than one covered with carpeting or an area rug. Both products are hard-wearing—an important consideration in this heavy-traffic area. Marble is also handsome and durable, but it is more costly to install. Wall-to-wall carpeting can be used equally well in a foyer; a solid color will do much to open up the floor area. If you decide to use wall-to-wall carpeting, select man-made fibers such as nylon or polyester; these wear well and are easy to spot clean and keep in pristine condition. If an area rug is your choice, then by all means use it; but it's wise to select one having pale colors and an open design to lighten the look at floor level.

Furniture that works well in a small foyer includes wall-hung pieces, scaled-down items, and objects made of see-through materials like glass with chrome or Plexiglas. Many manufacturers are producing wall-hung furniture specifically designed for a hall, such as a shelf-storage system that adds a furnished look, provides a spot for displaying attractive accessories—and frees much-needed floor space. Scaled-down items come in a fairly wide range; your best bets are narrow consoles, Parsons tables, slender chests, and simple chairs. Glass pieces and those made of clear plastic or Plexiglas are ideal because their transparent quality makes them appear to take up no space at all.

A cozy, boxlike effect is created through the use of vibrant, jewel-like colors, rich fabrics or wall coverings, or a luxurious carpet or area rug. However, since space is limited, it's a wise idea to use one basic color and material throughout for walls, ceiling, floor, and woodwork; accent colors can be introduced in accessories. Jewel-like colors that work well include ruby red, emerald green, sapphire blue, amethyst and garnet tones, or deep gold. Fabrics help to underscore the total effect when stapled to the walls; good choices are velvet, embossed velvet, silk, glazed cotton, synthetic suede or leather, wool, or felt. Cover the floor with either color-matched wall-to-wall carpeting or a modern, antique, or oriental area rug, depending on the style of the overall decorating scheme.

The same type of furniture just mentioned should be used in this type of decorative scheme, again because of its space-saving qualities. You can add to the handsomeness of the jewel-like foyer through the use of a good chandelier and wall candelabra, beautiful accessories, and plants. The latter can be ceiling-hung, grouped on the floor, or displayed on a piece of appropriate furniture. Highlight them with a spotlight.

Tips for an Awkwardly Shaped Foyer

An awkwardly shaped foyer can be treated in two ways. You can either camouflage its awkwardness through some clever decorating techniques or, alternatively, you can turn the unusual characteristics to advantage by playing them up. The easiest way to disguise the odd architectural elements that generally create an awkwardly shaped foyer is to paint the entire foyer a single solid color, including walls, ceiling, woodwork, and doors. In this way all of the unusual elements blend in and seem much less apparent. If you want to use a wall covering, select one in a solid color or with a simple, small-scale pattern that is not too dominant. Use the same technique, covering all areas with wall covering to create a smooth, unbroken, flowing quality and to marry odd architectural elements. If you don't want to cover the doors with the wall covering, paint them the same color as the background of the wall covering to produce a coordinated effect.

A floor covering that is color-matched to the walls will help to play down the awkward shape because this creates an unbroken flow of color and the eye is not stopped by contrasts. Vinyl tiles, wood, marble, and wall-to-wall carpeting in a man-made fiber are all good bets. An area rug sometimes makes the awkward shape seem all the more apparent. But if this is your preferred choice, select one that fits neatly into the center of the foyer so that it does not draw attention to odd wall jogs, niches, recesses, or other unusual architectural elements. Depending on the size and exact shape of the foyer, you can utilize square, oblong, or round area rugs.

Furniture can help to camouflage an awkward shape. For example, if a wall beam runs from floor to ceiling and cuts a wall in half, you can place furniture on either side of it. This technique helps to give a sense of balance to the area. You can use built-in bookshelves, two narrow étagères, or two slim, freestanding units on either side of the protruding beam. The beam will seem less apparent and the wall will look more even. If you don't have the space to use two of the above-mentioned items, or if your budget precludes buying two of them, select one piece to use on one side and a large plant or grouping of plants on the other to create the same effect. Examine the foyer carefully to pinpoint awkward areas and corners; try to find a piece of furniture that can be used in them to make the walls seem less broken up by these architectural elements. Wall-hung pieces or built-ins are your best bet, particularly since they help to free floor space and allow for traffic patterns.

If you feel that the odd characteristics in your awkwardly shaped foyer give it a certain personality, don't try to camouflage them. Instead, leave them as they are and let them make their own statement. You can even turn them to advantage by playing them up, so that they add to the decorative theme of the foyer. For instance, protruding wall beams can be covered with mirrors so that they become a glittering, eye-catching feature. You can use add-on architecture, such as wall and ceiling beams and molding to highlight architectural oddities and turn them into a conversation piece. Wall coverings and fabrics work in the same way. The products you select to give emphasis to these unusual elements naturally depend on the size of the foyer. Don't select any that will overpower it or make it look crowded.

When you are using this decorating technique, it's wise to keep the floor covering and furniture fairly simple and understated so that neither compete with the architecture. Utilize the same products mentioned earlier: wall-to-wall carpeting, vinyl tiles, wood, and area rugs for the floor; wall-hung furniture, freestanding wall systems, and small-scale items that don't overcrowd the space or halt the flow of traffic.

When there is **no entrance foyer at all,** and the front door opens directly into the living room, it is usually easier to dispense with the idea of creating a foyer. You can do this by simply making the area part of the living room, using the same decorative theme throughout.

Defining a Small Space as a Foyer

However, if there is a small amount of space between the front door and the living room that is perhaps narrower or of a different shape, you can give it a degree of definition as a foyer.

Here are some suggestions as to how you can do this effectively.

Cover the walls in the immediate vicinity of the door with a wall covering that contrasts with the one used in the living room to create a feeling of separateness. Vinyl, wallpaper, and fabric are all appropriate. But be sure the wall covering harmonizes with the walls beyond in terms of color, style, and pattern. A scenic or mural wallpaper utilized on one wall introduces a feeling of depth and three-dimensionality helping to visually open up the area. A mirrored wall produces the same effect. Alternatively, you can simply paint the walls in the door area a different color to create a sense of contrast and demarcation. Again, be sure the color of the paint is compatible with the living room color scheme.

Add-on architecture, when used with discretion, will define the area as a separate foyer. Strip molding run around the walls at ceiling and floor level is very effective, especially when painted a contrasting color. Or you can run the molding around the middle of the walls to create a chair-rail effect. Panels of trellis attached to one or two walls introduces architectural overtones as well as a visual change of pace. It also makes a good backdrop for plants, which can be arranged against it or suspended from it at different levels.

If you have used the same floor covering throughout the entire area, you might consider adding **a handsome rug** to define the door area as a foyer. Select a rug that fulfills the decorative scheme of the living room. Use a contemporary design if the room is modern and a traditional pattern if the scheme is period in style.

Accessories utilized on one or two walls are ideal in this area because they take up no floor space and introduce a visual change of pace and a bit of variety. Think in terms of a grouping of artworks, wall-hung brackets holding small decorative objects, a large mirror balanced on either side by candelabra, an arrangement of decorative china plates and wall plaques, a handsome clock, or a large wall hanging.

Lighting fixtures can be used to highlight the area and give it foyer mannerisms. Consider using a handsome chandelier of either modern or traditional design. For added interest and definition you can balance this with candelabra or sconces attached to the appropriate walls.

Certain pieces of furniture can be included in the doorway section of a room, but they should take up little floor space, and be correctly sized for the dimensions of the area. A small table placed against a wall under a mirror works well, as does a narrow console or Parsons table. If you prefer, select a small decorative chest that provides storage space and a display surface for accessories. Wall-hung pieces can also be utilized to advantage; they introduce life and movement when filled with accessories and plants. Placement of furniture is vital. If you are using freestanding pieces, be sure they do not block traffic patterns and are not in danger of being knocked over if they are lightweight.

To sum up, a foyer should always have a degree of decorative focus, be in step with the overall decorative mood of the entire apartment, and express your personal tastes.

The interesting use of mirrored surfaces does much to give this entrance in a duplex apartment its unique appearance. Mirrors have been utilized to cover pilasters in the hall, turning what were formerly architectural defects into a stunning focal point. The pilasters become sparkling columns that reflect light and objects within the area; they also expand the feeling of space. Additional strips of mirror were run up the end of the staircase wall to introduce a sparkling reflective quality. The staircase wall and the areas between the mirrored pilasters are lined with chocolate brown suede, creating an unusual play of textures. Underscoring this effect are such diverse textures as ceramic tile installed on the floor of the foyer, cleverly juxtaposed against the luxurious carpeting on the staircase. The designers used a combination of brown and white carpeting on the stairs. The white on the outer edge gives a floating look to the staircase, as does the banister made of lucite. This same material reappears in the pedestal that holds the handsome unicorn sculpture. The chandelier, which simulates antlers, illuminates the hall and offers a sparkling welcome to all who enter. This entrance was designed by *Camboy Interiors.*

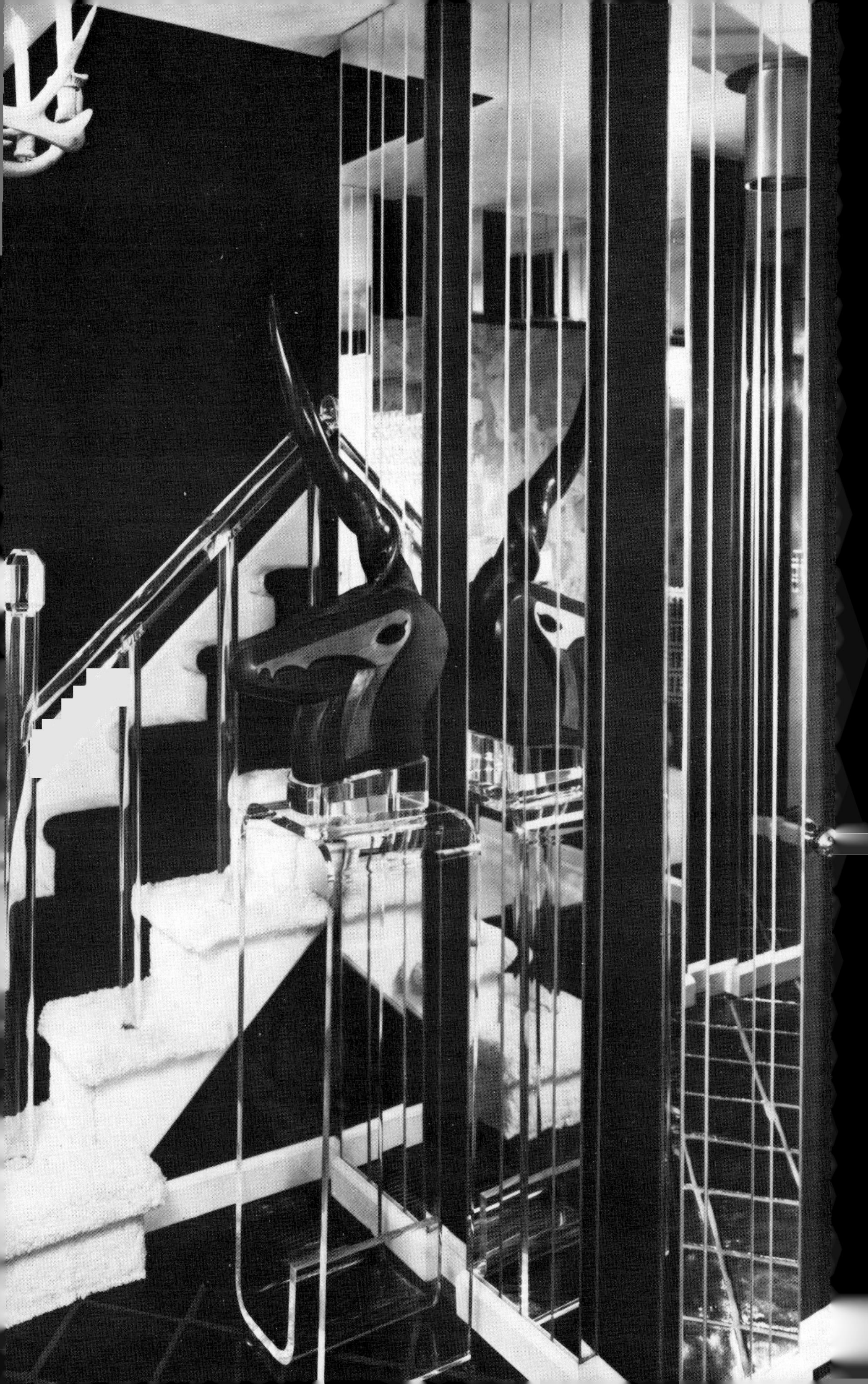

This entrance hall in the home of *June Gussin,* A.S.I.D., is typical of those found in many old apartments. In its original state two closets, one large and one small, broke up the wall space, making it difficult to create effective decorative wall treatments. Since it was also relatively narrow, it was not possible to furnish it with small pieces of furniture. After a careful analysis of the entrance, the designer decided not only to give it a furnished look with a colorful rug, plants, and accessories but also to utilize the space to the fullest by turning it into another room. She was able to do this by converting the large closet into an attractive bar, which makes the hall doubly useful.

The doors of the closet were removed, along with top shelves and the hanging rail. The interior of the closet was then covered with an attractive corklike wallpaper. Small shelves for glasses and a large mirror were added, along with a built-in base unit, to provide storage and counter space. Drawers hold all manner of bar utensils and linens; the cupboards below can be used to store bottles and extra crystal.

To introduce color, pattern, and texture to the entrance hall the designer selected a handsome area rug of Berber design. Apart from delineating the bar area, the pattern of the rug leads the eye into the living room beyond. The rug was anchored into position with nonskid tape—a point to remember when utilizing area rugs anywhere in your home, but especially in traffic ways. A traditional "library steps" table of just the right size was placed at the entrance to the living room, where it functions as a place for holding snack foods. Note how the skillful treatment gives the entrance greater importance and makes formerly wasted space function more practically for living needs.

THE FAMILY ALEC WAU
ANDROMEDA STRAIN
HUMAN ZOO by DESMOND MORRIS
Dennis Bloodworth
AND LOVE

In this narrow apartment entrance hall there was considerably more space on the walls than the floor. Designer *Peggy Walker* used one wall to great advantage, introducing handsome looks and practicality in the area through the addition of wall-hung cabinets and shelves, both of which were hand rubbed to preserve the natural beauty of the walnut. Nearly invisible brackets support the shelves, which provide space for an overflow of books from another room, a group of travel mementos, as well as greenery. Two four-drawer chests hold a multitude of things that need to be stowed away either for occasional or frequent use. Grooved drawers on the chests eliminate the need for hardware and give them a sleek look—as well as providing a bruise-free passageway. Since the unit floats well above the baseboard, cleaning the floor is easy. The system adds a furnished look without crowding and introduces a focal point in the entryway. Underscoring the unit as the center of eye interest is the colorful rug placed in front of it. A green and white wallpaper helps to open up the confined dimensions with its airy pattern. Lastly, ceiling lights provide the correct illumination.

A duplex apartment in a remodeled brownstone had a traditional foyer typical of this kind of dwelling. It was small, confined, dark, and lacking in any kind of architectural interest. Interior designer *Jane Victor,* A.S.I.D., tackled the light problem first. By adding a door with glass panels that permitted daylight to flow in, she counteracted the basic gloominess. She also selected a wall covering with a shiny background that reflects light and bounces it back into the foyer. This green and gold documentary pattern is ideal for the traditional mood of this home; it also serves as the perfect background for the antiques. To create a unified look the designer stayed with a basically monochromatic scheme, using green wall-to-wall carpeting in the hall, in the corridor leading to the kitchen and dining room, and for the staircase to the second floor. The green shell is highlighted with white paintwork. Because space was at a premium, *Jane Victor* settled for one dramatic piece of furniture, namely, the antique French commode topped with white marble, and gave added importance to this object by hanging a mirror and wall sconces above it. An old chest topped with a dark green leather seating pad was positioned on the opposite wall; it is completed by the plant and prints. Small green leather benches on either side of the antique commode complete the entrance, which is illuminated by a handsome chandelier.

Often a foyer has the mannerisms of a corridor, which may make it seem doubly difficult to decorate. This was the problem interior designer *Virginia Frankel,* A.S.I.D., faced when she moved into her new apartment. The entrance was long, narrow, and dark; it was also problematical in that it had one wall broken up by doors, a fuse box, and an intercom. *Virginia Frankel* began her decorative treatment by painting the ceiling and one wall white and staining the wood floor a dark mahogany. She then created a striped effect on the white wall to camouflage the fact that it was broken up by doors and other elements. Her method included the use of strips of gray patent vinyl wall covering cut in varying widths, which she ran from floor to ceiling on the difficult wall. As you can see, the closet door, the fuse box, and the intercom are all well integrated and much less apparent. The louvered door was painted white, but for continuity additional strips of gray patent vinyl were added to the end of the wall on the other side of the louvered door. The opposite wall was treated to a solid raft of gray vinyl. Because of space limitations, the designer used a minimum of furniture; these include the white Parsons table placed against the all-gray wall and a small chest next to the louvered door. These help to add a finished look, provide surface space for accessories, yet do not infringe too much on the floor space. Giving focus to the narrow hallway is the designer's lighting treatment. This consists of a set of ceiling track fixtures that provide plenty of illumination and highlight the striped wall most effectively. Incidentally, the type of treatment used here is relatively inexpensive to duplicate yourself. Select a vinyl that is color-matched to the overall scheme of your living room to create a feeling of continuity.

Very often a foyer can be turned into a functional living area through a little careful planning and clever decorating. This entrance hall, which opens directly into a living room, was given fresh dimensions and a whole new look through the inclusion of appropriate furniture and accessories, which turned it into a work corner. The owners selected lightly scaled furniture that fitted easily into the space. They purposely chose pieces of chrome and glass to help further the illusion of extra space as a result of their see-through qualities and shiny surfaces. The art deco-style desk is of chrome and glass, with brass inset on the legs. It is partnered by a shell chair with a chrome frame, upholstered in bright red nylon for durability. The wall behind the desk was lined with a silver-toned wall covering and a long shelf was added and covered with the same material. It serves as a handy counter for drinks and accessories. To give the entrance visual focus, an eye-catching wall hanging colored in black, white, green, and magenta was suspended from a brass rod. The same coffee-colored wall-to-wall carpeting used in the living room was carried into the entrance hall to create a feeling of continuity and a sense of unbroken space, helping to pull the entrance area into the living room. Yet at the same time the foyer retains its individuality through the clever choice and placement of furntiture and unique accessories that are well displayed. The desk doubles as a buffet server for large parties, as does the built-in shelf.

Often a foyer has the mannerisms of a corridor, which may make it seem doubly difficult to decorate. This was the problem interior designer *Virginia Frankel,* A.S.I.D., faced when she moved into her new apartment. The entrance was long, narrow, and dark; it was also problematical in that it had one wall broken up by doors, a fuse box, and an intercom. *Virginia Frankel* began her decorative treatment by painting the ceiling and one wall white and staining the wood floor a dark mahogany. She then created a striped effect on the white wall to camouflage the fact that it was broken up by doors and other elements. Her method included the use of strips of gray patent vinyl wall covering cut in varying widths, which she ran from floor to ceiling on the difficult wall. As you can see, the closet door, the fuse box, and the intercom are all well integrated and much less apparent. The louvered door was painted white, but for continuity additional strips of gray patent vinyl were added to the end of the wall on the other side of the louvered door. The opposite wall was treated to a solid raft of gray vinyl. Because of space limitations, the designer used a minimum of furniture; these include the white Parsons table placed against the all-gray wall and a small chest next to the louvered door. These help to add a finished look, provide surface space for accessories, yet do not infringe too much on the floor space. Giving focus to the narrow hallway is the designer's lighting treatment. This consists of a set of ceiling track fixtures that provide plenty of illumination and highlight the striped wall most effectively. Incidentally, the type of treatment used here is relatively inexpensive to duplicate yourself. Select a vinyl that is color-matched to the overall scheme of your living room to create a feeling of continuity.

Very often a foyer can be turned into a functional living area through a little careful planning and clever decorating. This entrance hall, which opens directly into a living room, was given fresh dimensions and a whole new look through the inclusion of appropriate furniture and accessories, which turned it into a work corner. The owners selected lightly scaled furniture that fitted easily into the space. They purposely chose pieces of chrome and glass to help further the illusion of extra space as a result of their see-through qualities and shiny surfaces. The art deco-style desk is of chrome and glass, with brass inset on the legs. It is partnered by a shell chair with a chrome frame, upholstered in bright red nylon for durability. The wall behind the desk was lined with a silver-toned wall covering and a long shelf was added and covered with the same material. It serves as a handy counter for drinks and accessories. To give the entrance visual focus, an eye-catching wall hanging colored in black, white, green, and magenta was suspended from a brass rod. The same coffee-colored wall-to-wall carpeting used in the living room was carried into the entrance hall to create a feeling of continuity and a sense of unbroken space, helping to pull the entrance area into the living room. Yet at the same time the foyer retains its individuality through the clever choice and placement of furntiture and unique accessories that are well displayed. The desk doubles as a buffet server for large parties, as does the built-in shelf.

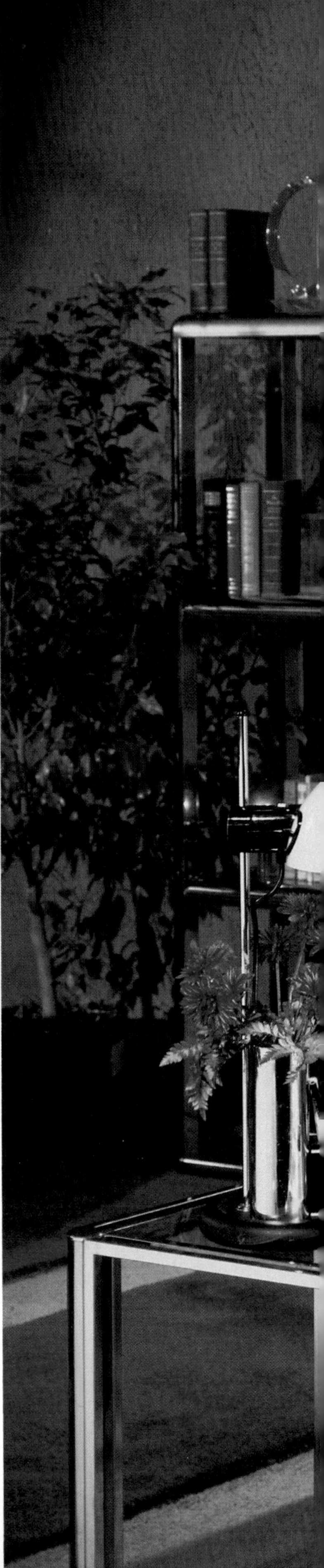

volume 67
GOHISCA

This foyer was so small and dull that it seemed to defy decoration. But imagination, ingenuity, a good wall covering, and a few pieces of scaled-down furniture gave it good looks, style, and that all-important focus. The decorating scheme began with the walls. These were covered with a vinyl wall covering that has the look of individual Mediterranean tiles. In point of fact, the wall covering comes in rolls and is easy to install yourself. Colored in rust and blue on a white ground, the wall covering introduces depth, dimension, color, and pattern. It also sets the mood for the other furnishings. The latter were kept relatively simple for space and budgetary reasons. A narrow shelf covered in a marblelike plastic laminate was a do-it-yourself project undertaken by the man of the house. Since it is wall-hung, it replaces the need for the traditional chest or console and provides surface space for appropriate accessories. It is balanced by a Spanish-style mirror and brackets holding candles, as well as two rush-seated stools below. A collection of plants and candles on metal holders add just the right finishing touch to this entrance, which is high on style and low in cost to create. Incidentally, the vinyl wall covering is washable and therefore easy to keep in pristine condition.

Designer *Peggy Walker* used some well-chosen accessories to give focus to a truly minuscule entrance. The only piece of furniture used is a butcher block Parsons table that holds most of the accessories. The designer began her scheme by painting the walls white; she then positioned the Parsons table so that it acted as a guideline for the wall treatment. This is easy for anyone to do. It consists of a simple super-graphic composed of an oval and a single straight line painted bright blue. Within the oval she hung a sculptured clock of solid oak with a white dial and burnt umber Roman numerals. Note how cleverly the straight line leads the eye to the clock, which gains additional importance from the bright blue oval surrounding it. Flower or plant holders made of bark, baskets, and a pewter pitcher complete the charming still life. Of course, the types of accessories you use will depend on your personal taste. This simple table lends itself to almost any decorative ornamentation. Because the little foyer opens directly into the living room, the table is used as an extra server. This setting proves how good looks can be created with very little expense.

The average apartment entrance hall is squared off and without any architectural elements to give it interesting overtones, making it appear impossible to decorate effectively and bring into focus. But interior designer *Margot Gunther,* A.S.I.D., proves the opposite in this typical foyer decorated in three different and distinctive ways to illustrate the eye-catching effects that can be produced. An interesting clock was the starting point for her decorating scheme. In each instance the finished result is an entrance with that all-important focus of decorative interest designed to appeal to individual tastes.

An elegant clock establishes an elegant mood in the first foyer. *Margot Gunther* accents the antique style of the long-case wall clock with an overall treatment that features wall panels, a skirted table, a lambrequin and shade at the door, which leads to a small terrace, plus an oriental area rug. Except for the rug, which, like the clock, is of heirloom quality, the furnishings are all inexpensive since this was designed as a do-it-yourself room. The designer began by hanging panels of wall covering on the walls, balancing wide panels with narrower ones. She then outlined each panel with carved wood molding to give the walls focus. The door was treated to a plywood lambrequin covered with the same wall covering, while the Austrian-style shade was made of a coordinated fabric. This same fabric was used to skirt the long table, an unfinished wood piece purchased from a home improvement center for very little. Vases, books, and other diverse accessories dress up the table. The vinyl wall covering and fabric set the color scheme, based on a play of harvest tones, which is repeated in the rug and the adjoining living room. The latter is furnished in a traditional style as well.

Designer *Margot Gunther* took an entirely different approach for her second decorating scheme for the same type of foyer. The contemporary theme stems from a school-day clock in a solid oak case with a natural oiled finish. The designer gave interest and focus to the walls by painting vibrant green, red, and orange stripes up and across a wall and a door, making the boxy, eight-foot-square foyer seem larger. Vinyl tiles repeat the green and red of the walls and serve as a border for the white vinyl floor. The made-to-measure vertical shade cloth blinds are also red and green; they control light, provide privacy, and are as adaptable to this narrow door as a whole window wall. Red fabric trimmed with green tape covers the valance above the blinds. With the basic shell completed, *Margot Gunther* hung the clock on the central wall and added a desk and canvas chair. Both pieces are of the assemble-it-yourself type of furniture. They help to transform the foyer into an office at home. The foyer echoes the modern mood of the adjoining living room.

The third type of foyer is period in feeling. As you can see, it can also double as an office when required while still being decorative. Once again the scheme begins with a clock. This long-drop regulator dates back to the 1700s. Equally fine and well scaled to the setting are a brass lamp and a sixty-inch worktable that can also be used as a sofa table or console. It is teamed with an Early American chair. The lattice at the window is a do-it-yourself project consisting of three-quarter-inch lath set in a white frame and highlighted by a brass planter holding ferns. The flooring is also a do-it-yourself product, a brick pattern in twelve-inch vinyl tiles that are easy to install yourself. The wall covering, a stucco-textured vinyl, is simple to hang and easy to keep in good condition through simple scrubbing.

REGULATOR

Functional Rooms for the Younger Set

Children need their own domain, especially in an apartment, where space is often at a premium. For general family harmony, it is desirable to create children's rooms that are totally self-contained and serve most of any child's living needs, whatever the age.

It is possible to create functional and adaptable rooms for the younger set through good planning, a careful choice of the latest furniture, and products that are attractive, durable, and can also grow with the child.

Begin by making a floor plan of the room, utilizing the previously mentioned method. The floor plan will enable you to plan furniture arrangements properly for the best utilization of available space. It will also show you just how many pieces you can comfortably include and will act as a buying guide when you start to decorate.

Once you have made your floor plan, investigate the latest products for walls and floor so that you can develop a scheme for the basic shell. Apart from good looks, these materials should be practical, durable, and easy to maintain, since children's rooms do take lots of wear and tear. If they provide soundproofing as well, this is an added advantage since it ensures comfort and greater privacy for the rest of the household.

Checklist of Products for Walls and Floors

Lots of products are now available that add decorative flair to a child's room in combination with the practical qualities just mentioned. All of them are widely distributed across the country and are relatively inexpensive. Many of them lend themselves to do-it-yourself decorating schemes if this is an important budgetary consideration.

Vinyl wall covering is undoubtedly a good buy, since it has a variety of built-in qualities that make it ideal for use in a child's room. Because of their weight, most vinyls add a degree of soundproofing. All of them camouflage marred walls, thus eliminating the costly job of replastering surfaces. Since the majority are pretrimmed, prepasted, and strippable, they are a cinch to put up; you therefore save the cost of installation, which can be high because of the labor involved. Vinyl wall covering is extremely durable—a vital quality for children's rooms. It withstands most spots and staining, and is hygienic because it can be cleaned easily with soap and water when sticky fingerprints or surface dust has to be removed.

Manufacturers are producing vinyl wall covering in charming patterns designed to delight the eye of the child. You can choose almost anything, from depictions of old nursery rhymes and comic-book characters to stylized patterns relating to nature and animals. Colors are generally bright, cheerful, and cleverly blended to create highly original effects. Some vinyls come with a coordinated wall covering having the same coloration but featuring only one element of a pattern. The coordinated material can be used on the ceiling and doors to introduce lively effects. Also, many vinyls have coordinated fabrics. These can be used for window and bed treatments to introduce a custom-designed look. This is a good techique to use, especially if space is limited, since utilization of one pattern throughout helps to expand the feeling of space.

Paint is a practical product to use in a child's room. It is not all that costly, a wide range of bright colors are readily available, and it is easy to keep in pristine condition through soap-and-water cleaning. However, it does not introduce any soundproofing, nor does it hide marred wall surfaces. Nevertheless, interesting effects can be created with paint. For instance, walls can be flashed with one color, with a contrasting color appearing on the ceiling and doors. Supergraphics can be splashed across walls and up onto the ceiling in imaginative ways that appeal to the young.

Wood paneling is a good choice for a child's room for a number of reasons. It hides poor walls, introduces superb soundproofing, is highly durable and not easily damaged, and is simple to keep clean. Light wood tones are most suitable since they are "younger" in feeling and also help to stretch space by means of visual illusion. Some wood paneling looks better painted, particularly planking, and this is worth considering. An alternative is decorator paneling that simulates wood and comes in a variety of vivid colors bound to please children, who naturally tend to favor bright tones.

Now let's examine some of the best products to use on the floor of a child's room.

Vinyl tiles are most popular today—and with good reason. They are not expensive, colors and patterns are endless, they are hard-wearing, and they're maintenance-free. They mop clean in a jiffy, require no waxing to keep their sheen, and they are difficult to damage. Any number of eye-catching designs can be created through the use of contrasting color combinations or unusual placement of differently colored tiles. Checkerboard effects, patchwork patterns, stripes, and abstract designs are not that hard to create, and all introduce unique decorative touches. It is a wise idea to add a large area rug when vinyl tiles have been used for the overall flooring. A rug provides warmth, comfort, and some degree of soundproofing, as well as an extra decorative look. Always be sure the rug is well anchored with skid-free tape to avoid accidents.

Carpeting has lots of advantages for a child's room. First and foremost, it adds warmth, comfort, and it cushions falls. It also has good soundproofing qualities. Carpets consisting of man-made fibers are the best to use in a child's room because they are hard-wearing and easy to spot clean or shampoo. Wall-to-wall carpeting helps increase the spaciousness of the floor area most effectively, especially when it is a solid color. However, certain patterned carpets show less dirt and soiling and should therefore be considered. If you are working on a limited budget, look at the latest carpet tiles, which are less costly than broadloom. Because they have a self-adhesive backing, they are simple to install.

Wood floors are certainly hard-wearing in a child's room, but they offer little comfort or warmth when left bare. They obviously do not provide soundproofing either. For these reasons it is wise to add a good-sized area rug or a piece of broadloom carpeting cut to area rug size and bound at the edges. Again, always be sure the rug is well anchored into position with tape to avoid skids and falls. A wood floor can either be left in its natural state or painted a light or bright color, depending on personal preference. Several coats of polyurethane should be added to protect the paint from scuffs and stains. If you want to be really inventive, consider stenciling gay patterns onto the painted floor.

Window Treatments that Work

Light control is vital in a child's room. You should therefore plan your window treatments with care. Essentially, a successful treatment provides a degree of privacy, room-darkening qualities when required, good flow of natural light, and decorative overtones.

Window shades have a lot to offer. Raised during the day, they permit light to enter; pulled down at night, they darken the room. They are not very expensive, are easy to install within the window frame, and can be kept pristine with weekly sponging. They work extremely well in combination with draperies, a lambrequin, or shutters; alternatively, they can also be used alone. Window shades lend themselves to all manner of decorative treatments. They can be trimmed with fancy braid, highlighted with decals or fabric cutouts, treated to stenciled patterns, or laminated with a fabric that matches draperies or upholstery. There is a wide range of colors to choose from that will blend with almost any color scheme.

Vertical blinds are fresh and clean-looking for a child's room. They can be made to fit any size window and provide superb light control during the day, room-darkening qualities at night, and privacy at all times. The vanes are simply angled to produce the desired amount of light or shade in a room. They look their best when used alone.

Narrow-slatted blinds have superseded venetian blinds. They are another good choice for a child's room, since they provide necessary light control, privacy, and fit neatly within the window frame. Since they come in a wide range of decorator colors, they introduce the most lively effects; various combinations of colors can be used to create striped effects that are eye-catching and different. They can be used in combination with draperies but also look good surrounded by a lambrequin. Lastly, they can be cleaned easily.

Lined draperies provide room-darkening qualities at night and permit the flow of light during the day. If you plan on utilizing these, select a style that is in keeping with the overall decorative mood of the room. Select a fabric that can be repeated on upholstered pieces or used in a bed treatment and thereby avoid too many busy patterns in the room. When choosing your drapery fabric, it's a good idea to look at those that have been specially treated to withstand soiling and staining in order to cut down on dry-cleaning bills.

You can use draperies in combination with window shades, narrow-slatted vertical blinds, or lightweight sheer curtains that hang close to the glass.

Furniture Suggestions

There are several things to consider when selecting furniture for a child's room.

1. The pieces should be of the right scale to suit the size of the room. Avoid large bulky pieces if the room is small; seek out small-scale items that help to conserve space. You have more leeway in a room of large proportions and can utilize items that are more generously scaled. Avoid very small pieces, as these will look lost in a large space.

2. The materials the furniture is made of should be durable and not easily damaged. Sturdy woods are your best bet, although some plastic pieces are hard-wearing. In particular, avoid glass items in a child's room for obvious reasons.

3. Whenever possible, pick furniture that is devoid of sharp corners and edges to lessen the chance of the child being hurt. Look for pieces that have rounded corners, smooth edges, and unadorned legs.

4. Select a style that will "grow" with the child. In other words, don't buy furniture that will look too childish in a few years and will therefore be outdated. Instead, pick items that will wear well through infancy and the toddler stages up into the teen years. A wide range of suitable furniture is available to choose from that weathers the years, so this is not as difficult as it sounds.

DOUBLE-DUTY FURNITURE

Double-duty furniture is a boon in children's rooms because it is such a space saver. It is also economical as well as practical. There are all manner of double-duty pieces on the market, all of which help a child's domain live up to its basic function. A Parsons table is perfect because it can serve so many purposes. It works as a desk, a place for meals, a counter for games or painting, and a display surface for toys and other juvenile possessions. It has no age limit in that it will always function well as a desk, dining counter, or dressing table in later years. Parsons tables are available in a variety of woods, painted finishes, or plastic laminate finishes.

Hinged cubes serve a variety of functions. They can act as occasional tables for games, snacks, or displaying toys. The interior provides extra storage space for items that are bulky. Even nonseasonal clothes can be tucked way in them. Like the Parsons table, they are available in all manner of wood tones and finishes; some are made of sturdy plastic in a range of vibrant colors.

The trundle bed is ideal to use in a child's room that is short on space. The lower bed simply slides out when the child has an overnight guest. Since the lower bed is out of the way during daytime hours, the trundle-style bed frees central floor space most of the time. If the trundle bed is not to your preference, consider bunk beds. Because these stack up the wall instead of extending out into the floor area, a minimum amount of space is utilized to the utmost.

In a teenager's room the sofa bed truly comes into its own. The perfect space saver, it helps to introduce sitting room mannerisms into the area by day. At night it opens up into a comfortable bed. In the past few years designs have been improved upon and engineering really refined. All kinds of styles and sizes are available to suit individual decorative schemes and room dimensions.

WALL-HUNG FURNITURE

Wall-hung furniture can be used to great advantage in rooms for the younger set, helping to make them functional and adaptable around the clock. Obviously, wall-hung furniture frees floor space for games and other pastimes; it also allows you to include other pieces of furniture. Manufacturers are making good-looking wall systems designed to last many years. A set of open shelves in combination with storage cabinets set high and low is a wise investment, as are units that come with drop-leaf desk tops that do double-duty as work and snack counters. Books, toys, and other juvenile possessions can be well displayed on the open shelves, while the cabinets provide much-needed storage space for clothes, linens, games, sports equipment, and records.

If these ready-made wall systems are out of your price range, you can create your own. *Jane Victor,* A.S.I.D., recommends using some unfinished wood items for a wall-hung unit that functions as a work center. She will hang a set of open shelves on a wall and then balance the shelves with a counter top attached to the wall with brackets. She has explained that the counter top must be approximately eighteen inches wide to provide an adequate work surface. However, the counter can be any length you want, provided it is scaled to the length of the shelves to create a balanced look. Shelves can be painted or lacquered in the desired color; the counter top should be covered with a color-matched plastic laminate for durability. The counter also doubles as a convenient snack area.

Storage Solutions

As often as not, there is insufficient storage space in a child's room. There are a variety of ways to provide extra storage areas that are not difficult to accomplish. Here are some suggestions from leading designers.

Janet Shiff suggests running a series of open shelves from floor to ceiling on one wall. The central portion of the shelves should be filled with books, toys, and possessions in everyday use. The highest and lowest shelves should be utilized as storage space. Since items to be stored cannot be on view, Janet selects attractive Far Eastern baskets to hold these items. She arranges the largest baskets on the bottom shelves and the smaller baskets on the top shelves. If you prefer, select decorative boxes from the closet shop in a department store and use them in place of baskets. These create an especially pretty effect in a girl's room.

Leif Pedersen, A.S.I.D., makes doors work overtime in a child's room, be it one occupied by a boy or a girl. His technique is to utilize all manner of closet accessories that can be attached to the inside of the door. His suggestions include: a shoe bag suspended from a strong hook to free floor space in the closet for attractive boxes that hold sweaters, nonseasonal clothes, and bed linens; plastic caddies attached to the inside of the door with adhesive, ranged in a line from top to bottom, to house all manner of items, including cameras, games, magazines, and stereo tapes; three sets of tie racks to be used for such items as belts, scarves, hair ribbons, as well as ties. If hanging space is at a premium, Leif recommends the twelve-inch hanging rod that screws into the door and extends into the closet itself. This will hold as many as twelve lightweight items on hangers.

John Elmo, A.S.I.D., often utilizes a series of oriental picnic-style baskets to provide extra storage for clothes and linens. John selects baskets in graduated sizes and stacks them on top of each other in a corner of the room. Apart from being practical, they also add decorative overtones, are lightweight, and are easy to handle.

Joan Blutter, F.A.S.I.D., points out that space under the bed is often wasted. She suggests using large decorative boxes under the bed for storing blankets, linens, and items not in everyday use. The boxes are inexpensive and easy to lift, since they are made of cardboard. They come in all sizes, are flat enough to be pushed under the bed, and are available in the closet shop of most department stores.

Joyce Vagasy likes to see juvenile possessions on view if they are attractive enough. To this end she will cover a large portion of a wall with pegboard painted a bright color or one that ties in with the decorative scheme. All manner of objects can be hung on the pegboard. They are also within easy reach of the child.

Color Works Magic

An attractive color scheme is important in any room of an apartment, especially in the child's domain. Almost all children love bright, gay colors; they often they have definite preferences.

Before creating a color scheme for a child's room, it's a good idea to sound out the child on his or her preferences so that you can utilize colors the child feels happy being around. However, it must also be a scheme that you know the child will not tire of quickly, one that has a decent life-span. Some color schemes are simply too juvenile to weather the years; you cannot keep redoing the room because the child is bored with the scheme or has outgrown it. Be selective and compromise so that everyone is pleased.

Before putting your color plan into operation, remember some of the facts about color discussed earlier and the tricks they play. To refresh your memory, here they are again.

1. Light and pastel colors recede and therefore help to visually expand the space in a room.

2. Dark or bright colors advance into a room and so reduce the spaciousness by visual illusion.

3. Light falling on any colored surface changes the intensity of the color, making it look brighter or darker. Pay attention to the natural daylight entering the room and establish its direction to better understand the effects it will produce.

4. Northern and eastern daylight is cold, making cool colors look colder than they really are. Western and southern light is warm and therefore makes hot colors look more fiery.

5. Color changes hue when used on a large expanse of a single wall or on several walls. For example, one wall painted red can be an eye-catching focal point. If the four walls of a room are painted red, they can look overpowering and far too hot and intense. Dark blue and fir green can produce gloomy effects when used throughout, while white can appear cold and sterile.

A variety of different color schemes appeal to children. Here are some that work well in rooms having various decorative styles. All have a reasonable life-span of several years, weather with ease, and generally don't become banal with constant viewing.

Red, white, and blue is particularly popular with boys. It's a scheme that lends itself to many treatments. But be sure you include plenty of white in accents to cool the red and blue and produce a balanced effect.

Pink and green is favored by girls. A stunning look can be introduced if you select a fairly deep pink or rose, as opposed to pastel pink, and apple green. Again, it's wise to balance these two colors with white for the best results.

Yellow and green accented by orange is popular with boys and girls. This combination creates a lovely, sunny, cheerful feeling in a room of any size. Let the yellow dominate, make green the second color, and use orange as the accent color. White can again be added as a second accent.

Other color combinations suitable for children's rooms include:

Yellow and white; yellow and green; yellow and blue

Green and orange; green and blue; green and coral

Blue and white; blue and brown; blue and orange

White and red; white and green; white and orange. In fact, white works well with any other color and is especially effective when it is balanced with a second color plus black.

Possessions Add Personality

A final word about the decoration of a child's domain. Not all children's possessions need to be hidden from view. In fact, it is possible to use many of them to add personality as well as a degree of decorative impact to a scheme. However, they should be arranged with flair and skill so that they do not produce a messy, cluttered look.

To this end, think of displaying toys and books on étagères or bookshelves; the latter can either be freestanding or wall-hung. Create interesting arrangements of juvenile memorabilia so that they make a statement about the room's occupant. You can display these on units, window ledges, shelves, or hang them on the wall, depending on the particular item. The main thing is to let the child's personality, tastes, and preferences shine forth.

OVERLEAF Imaginative ideas designed to delight any child give this youngster's haven a unique look. It is also a boon for adults, since it requires little care. The large room shown here is situated at one end of an old-fashioned apartment. (The ideas can be adapted to any size room by making shelf units smaller.) Probably first in importance to the potential occupant would be the marvelous, mosquito-netted tent. The tent and tent frame can easily be constructed over a weekend by an incurable do-it-yourselfer. Inside are two folding cots, mattresses, down comforters, and portable camp stools for night table use. There are also convenient battery operated lights—definitely an electricity-saving device. Featured along the lower wall is the illusion of growing grass created by the application of a cutout border made of a leaf print linen fabric. The floor covering, a mottled, gravel-patterned linen fabric in varying shades of beige, suggests a desert locale. A polyurethane finish, used here, is recommended when fabric is commandeered for use as heavy-duty floor covering. Other elements that make this child's place memorable include: fiber glass boulders stationed by the tent; red tractor-seat stools; industrial shelving to hold a mixture of toys, paraphernalia, balls, and books; a color spectrum of red, yellow, green, and blue linen-wrapped bulletin boards. At right angles to the shelving structure a long study counter extends along the wall. Accessible on another wall are hooks for hanging coats, sweaters, and Windbreakers.

Crayola

If at all possible, it is important to give a younger member of the family a room of her own, a space where she can follow her own pursuits and hobbies and satisfy (within reason) her own tastes in decoration. Feminine in feeling and essentially simple to execute, this room would be suitable for a young girl who likes traditionally dainty effects expressed through modern adaptations. Various shades of blue and white create a fresh and lovely haven. A crownlike canopy has been made by deftly sewing and suspending shimmering dark blue fabric from the ceiling. A paler blue polished cotton is draped from the small canopy in such a fashion that it forms a four-poster-style bed. The latter is covered in the dark blue fabric and a medium blue fabric is utilized for the dust ruffle. Pillows made of different fabrics are strewn on the bed, creating a lively mélange of color and pattern. Shag carpeting containing several shades of blue underscores the furnishings and is the perfect partner for the stylized floral vinyl wall covering. The furniture, bed, armoire, and commode are white with light and dark blue trim. NEXT PAGE A feeling of larger space is suggested through the use of a mirror on one wall, flanked on either side by built-in closets. A Roman blind in the window section defines the vanity area. Glass shelves hold a collection of antique dolls and further express the youngster's taste. Designed by *Jane Victor,* A.S.I.D.

MILLIONS OF CATS

OVERLEAF Nurture a budding dress designer by giving her a bedroom/sewing center of her very own. This double-duty room takes into account visual stimulation by using bright yellow, red, white, and blue accents. A charming print wall covering with a coordinated fabric envelops the entire space and sets the gay, cheerful mood. FOLLOWING PAGES Sleep and sitting space is provided for by the sofa, covered in a bright yellow corduroy upholstery fabric, which opens up into a bed. Storage is built into cabinets, bookcases, and file cabinets. Shirred fabric set into the louvers softens the angles and produces a coordinated window treatment. Everything has its place. Clothes and personal effects are stored away in a built-in closet at the far end of the area (not visible), while the sewing machine, thread, fabrics, and necessary notions are stored on shelves on an adjacent wall. The wall covering is also used to cover the cabinet doors and the trunk, which serves as a coffee table and provides additional storage for fabrics. Using one pattern throughout enlarges the space and gives it a "pulled together" look. The fresh appearance is easy to maintain because all the furnishings chosen are totally maintenance-free, including the bright red nylon carpeting.

SINGER

GIFT RIBBON
PARAMOUNT FABRICS CORP.
Velvets - Velveteens
Piques
125 W. 37th St.
N. Y. 18, N. Y.
Wisconsin 7-1526-7-8
NEEDLEWORK
RIBBON
BUTTONS
PATCHWORK SCRAPS
CROCHET
BEADS

THE VOGUE SEWING BOOK
Butterick
Simplicity
BEADS
CHALK-
PENCILS
thank

AMERICA
Jonathan

Fortunately, interior designer *Abbey Darer,* A.S.I.D., understands psychology as well as interior design. She knows that the best way to keep peace in a bedroom shared by two active boys is to give each his own territorial rights. That was the technique she used in this long, narrow room with a window at each end. She created two separate areas containing two bunk beds and a work corner under each window. (Only one end of the room is visible. The unseen portion is a mirror image of this photo.) She started by paneling the walls with prefinished birch. The bunk bed wall unit that divides the room was treated to the same durable quarter-inch-thick paneling. Then each newly made area, boasting its own window, was deftly turned into a private, study/hobby corner with tangerine plastic shelves laid across a pair of filing cabinets painted a paler orange. Room-darkening vinyl shades were set within each of the white-framed windows to provide tailored light control. Their bright yellow plays off beautifully against the paneling and picks up the color cue made by the bedspreads. To make it clear who is in possession where, each shade sports an individual graphic highlighting the occupant's name. The lettering is in the same royal blue of the hardy indoor/outdoor carpeting and the design around it is in the bright tangerine of the desk tops. Even though the bunk units are two-tiered for sleep-over friends, the paneled divider/wall does not go all the way up to the ceiling. Space was left for proper air and heat flow.

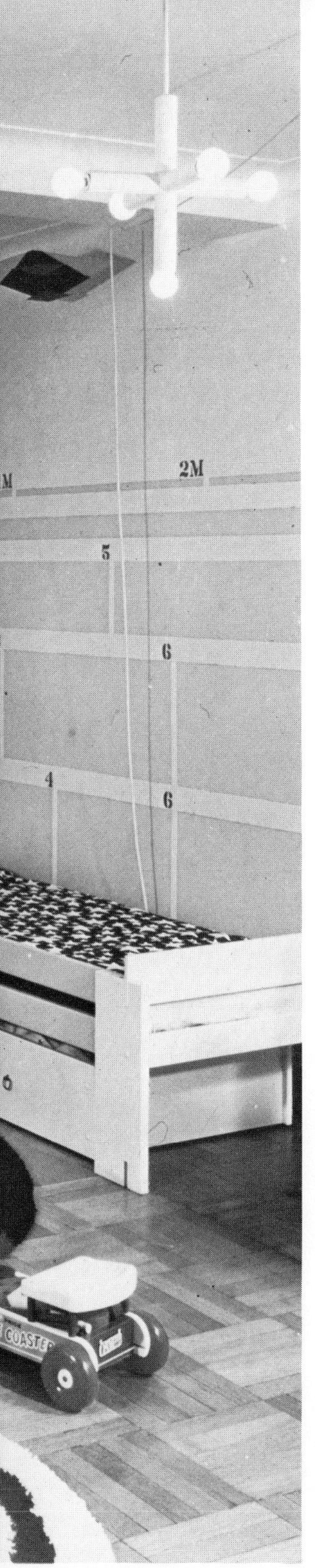

Wit, whimsy, and practicality all combine in this bed/playroom for a growing youngster. Designed by *Susan Grant Lewin,* it was skillfully decorated to adapt to the changing needs of a growing child over a period of years. The wood parquet floor in warm honey tones is practical, easy to care for, and hygienic. White walls and ceiling create a fresh, pristine mood. The bed wall is enlivened by a yellow painted-on "yardstick" that adds visual interest. Color is evident everywhere, but it is well controlled for a smooth, harmonious look. The fabric laminated onto window shades is a brilliant poster print combining yellow, red, black, and white. It helps to give the old-fashioned double-hung windows a new and exciting dimension. The shades have room-darkening qualities—a must in a youngster's domain. The room is spacious enough to allow for games and playtime activities as well as sleeping. Lighting is provided by two white chandeliers that share ceiling space with colorful, whimsical Japanese kites. Accessories have been selected with an eye to keeping the child amused.

OVERLEAF Bright, colorful, and cheery is a most apt description of this contemporary-style child's room designed by *Abbey Darer,* A.S.I.D., which is also high on practicality. Either a boy or a girl could be happy in this bedroom situated in a remodeled brownstone apartment. Two different yet color-related wall coverings set the stage. A stylized pattern composed of a house surrounded by trees and encircled by a rainbow covers one wall; the others are covered in a graphic print containing the word "rainbow," which was installed diagonally for added visual interest. Primary colors—red, green, yellow, blue—on white complete the color scheme. The bed/seating platform, upholstered in bright yellow, is accented with lots of multicolored pillows that fulfill the color scheme. Drawers located beneath the bed are color-keyed; they provide necessary storage areas for clothes and toys and help to make the most of the small space. The desk is actually a long board that extends from one end of the room to the other; it rests on the bed and also covers an unsightly radiator. Marigold carpeting in an easy-care fiber allows the child to play on the floor at any time and is simple to sponge clean. A molded plastic table and stools are highly practical and perfect for drawing and painting. They can be cleaned easily and can just as easily be moved around to accommodate guests or a change of activities. This is a truly wonderful setting to stimulate a child's creativity and develop an appreciation of order.

RAINBOW

RAINBOW

Although the space and budget for a child's room may be limited, careful planning and proper selection of products can do wonders. The small-scale pattern of this wall covering depicts charming bonneted little girls. It covers the walls of this small but enchanting place. Soft green, yellow, and brown on white are the colors that create the restful mood. A four-poster with a bookcase/headboard painted yellow is complemented by a bright yellow and white gingham coverlet. Natural caning covers the molding around the top of the bed, the drawers below, plus the headboard itself, creating unity and textural interest. Gingham fabric pillows in different colors increase the visual interest of the bed area. Books, vases, and pictures are stored in the headboard, which is a great space saver. A yellow rattan end table holds a small jewelry chest and other accessories. A coordinated fabric has been used to make the three-tiered cafe curtains at the window as well as to upholster a rocking chair adjacent to the window (not visible). A rattan chest and a small closet situated just outside the room provide ample storage in addition to under-the-bed storage.

A boy's room is bound to take a lot of rough-and-tumble play, so it's a good idea to give him as much free floor space as possible. That is why bunk beds are the most sensible and practical choice, especially when space is limited. This functional bedroom is done up in attractive "masculine" colors bound to appeal to a boy. The predominantly blue and green plaid carpet with yellow accent is coordinated with the matching striped thin-slat blinds to establish the basic scheme. Built-in bookcases frame the bunk bed and create lots of extra shelf space for treasured items. The wood-frame bed is painted royal blue to echo the carpet and to blend in with the back wall. Camel-colored down-filled comforters add an extra color accent of paler yellow that harmonizes with the basic scheme. Bunk beds are ideal for an overnight guest, too, but at most they provide for only one additional person. When a child wants to have more than one friend sleep over, a down-filled sleeping bag can be brought out. This rolls up and can be stored on a shelf or in a closet. This scheme can easily be adapted to meet a girl's needs by a mere change of accessories and a new color scheme.

OVERLEAF Interior designer *Vladimir Kagan* was given carte blanche to create a teenager's haven for a girl. He approached the idea with zestful know-how. After studying her tastes and interests, he divided—and, at the same time, unified—the room within a cleverly constructed framework, producing wonderful multipurpose living quarters. Birch plywood faces one side of the window wall and flows into a deep cornice that connects with a bookcase on the other side, in turn becoming part of the sofa bed niche. Then the birch continues on its way to act as a divider between the sleeping area and the built-in dresser/desk section in an open-plan manner. Functioning as a smashing accent that aids and abets this division, tieback curtains and a matching laminated shade add a gorgeous, floral splash of emerald green and Siamese pink at the windows. This vivacious decorative point is repeated on the spread and bolsters; the wall behind the bed was painted the dashing Siamese pink of the print. Underfoot an emerald green shag rug echoes the other strong color and ties the various segments of the whole together.

BETSY
LOGAN'S
LOGAN'S
THE TITANS
ENAMELLING
VALENTINE'S DAY

A child's bedroom or nursery is now receiving more attention for its value in developing a love of learning and beauty in a growing child. It is a project worthy of your time and energy. Pale woods and bright colors, coupled with easy-care finishes, make this hideaway designed by *Carol Mancione* a practical and attractive playroom. The walls are vivid yellow; the graphic above the fireplace is yellow, flame red, and chocolate; the tabletop and the Finnish chair seats are bright red. The yellow shaggy nylon plush carpet helps to pull all of these colors together to produce an integrated look. It is tough, long-wearing, and easy to maintain in tip-top condition. A child can sit, sleep, or roll around on it. According to the designer, children like a structure they can crawl or climb into; to this end she designed a playhouse, which is positioned next to the door. Painted navy, sun yellow, and white, it lends added interest to this fun room for a growing youngster. Anyone can make it out of plywood once the design has been drawn on it. The design is then cut out with a jigsaw. Next, it is primed, painted, and held together with screws and small metal brackets. Another major element is convenient storage—a must in a child's room, where it is important to introduce a semblance of order. The plastic rolling cart in the foreground has lots of drawers, some of which swing out; it is ideal for housing all manner of items and makes them easily accessible to the young occupant.

ABCDE
FGHIJK
LMNOP
QRSTU
VWXYZ

You can create a haven for a girl's growing years such as the one shown here. It is feminine and fresh, has lots of visual interest, and is easy to care for. The fabric used is the basis for the turquoise, pink, and white color scheme that predominates. Utilizing the same print everywhere enlarges the feeling of space and creates an orderly ambience. Turquoise carpeting underscores and pulls together all the other elements, such as the pink bedspread and chest, the prints on the walls, and the turquoise shutters. A practical white circular table, chairs, and small Parsons table, all made of plastic, were selected because there is no danger of chips or scratches. All are easy to clean; crayon, paint, and spills can be wiped up with a damp cloth. The carpet, which consists of a man-made fiber, is durable, maintenance-free, and introduces luxury underfoot. The skirted bed acts as a spot for storage through the use of special boxes that slide under it and hold nonseasonal clothes and other items. A built-in closet, whose doors are covered in the same fabric, lines a third wall. In general, space is organized in such a way as to produce order effortlessly.

Imaginative ideas guaranteed to appeal to a youngster spark this fun playroom situated at one end of a spacious juvenile bedroom (the sleeping area is not visible). The bright red carpeting that runs throughout introduces comfort, warmth, soundproofing, and also cushions falls. It is balanced and cooled by white walls and ceiling highlighted by splashes of yellow. Adding great visual interest is a three-dimensional mural on the contrasting blue wall. The wooden steps-and-slide structure is placed on yellow vinyl-covered foam pads to cushion falls; it is a fun addition for the young occupant and friends. A yellow beanbag chair and yellow and red barrel stools provide seating, while a giant bulletin board helps to create a painting area. A shelf fitted below holds paints and brushes. Toys displayed around the room contribute extra visual interest, as do the windows, which were treated to stick-on plastic decals depicting nursery rhyme characters. As the child matures, this end of the room can easily be converted into a work/study area through the simple removal of the structure and the addition of appropriate furniture.

Children love to be stimulated by bright colors and want to vent all that marvelous energy by running, jumping, and climbing. *Deborah A. Kunstler,* A.S.I.D., designed this fun-and-games room for both. It is full of great ideas. A mirrored ceiling enlarges the space by visual illusion, reflecting the curves and angles of the patterns on the stenciled floor and the super-graphics on the walls. The enormous old-fashioned window gains contemporary overtones through the addition of a white plywood lambrequin. Children can climb onto the window seat; the ledge is padded and upholstered in a silvery vinyl that matches the window blinds, which close or open to permit air to flow and the view to be seen. The bed, which was designed to incorporate storage space and a pull-out bunk, also includes a second-story sleep area. Painted white, it provides another area that the children can climb up into and play. The black-on-white "area rug" was painted on the floor surface, as was the white arrow "graphic" on the red-patent vinyl wall covering. Red is echoed in the storage modulars as well as the chairs. All surfaces can be wiped clean quickly, the room generally being maintenance-free.

OVERLEAF Because space was limited in this girl's room, a total unit was built in along the wall to provide storage at both ends and an alcove for the bed. The latter consists of a mattress that rests on a high wooden base, which was treated to a tailored spread made of white cotton eyelet and matching pillow shams. The facing of the plywood unit was painted shocking pink, which echoes one of the colors in the floral vinyl wall covering. The latter is splashed across all the walls, lines the alcove, and is also used to cover the hinged doors of the built-in closets (only one visible). A wooden valance was added across the entire built-in unit for a finished look. This is covered with a cream and white vinyl in an open trellis pattern. Other good ideas in this practical and pretty room are such things as the hooks on the end unit to hold possessions, a wall-hung shelf underneath the mirror, and concealed lighting behind the alcove's valance. A dressing-table shelf is serviced by a metal clothes hamper freshened by white paint and colored ribbons and topped by a seat made of wood and covered in moss green silk. The same green is repeated in the wall-to-wall carpeting, composed of a man-made fiber that is durable and easy to maintain, as is the washable vinyl wall covering. Apart from freeing floor space, the built-in unit helps to keep the room neat and uncluttered. The same ideas can be adapted for a boy's room.

D
DOT
Records

Color is the catalyst in this rather sophisticated yet tailored bedroom designed for a sixteen-year-old, a budding graphics artist. Designer *Peggy Walker* used an unusual combination of light to deep purples played off against the bright red bed wall and highlighted by occasional touches of orange. White, which is utilized on the ceiling, the other walls, and in the window area, provides a cooling effect in the vibrant shell. A pair of felt-covered bulletin boards create a super-graphic effect on the red wall; they also serve as backdrops for the bed and a modern cantilevered chair and ottoman. The violet-toned upholstery of the seating is color coordinated with the deep purple painted bed base and the narrow-slatted blinds at the window. This underscores the clean-lined look of the room and fits neatly within the frame. The window wall accommodates a series of low bookshelves topped by a counter that anchors the bookcase and radiator, creating a neat pulled-together look. Zingy plaid bed linens are in pink and violet tones, while the area rug is shaded in purple and red to fulfill the basic theme. A drop-leaf desk provides study/work space plus a place for snacks. The teenager's decorative interests and personal tastes are conveyed through the various accessories displayed on the window wall and the bulletin board.

scan
STAY ALIVE
AUTOBACKGAMMON
THE GAME OF GO
Apple Pie Knitter
MONOPOLY

Ideas for One-Room Apartments

Many first "homes" begin as a one-room apartment. This might be so if you are striking out on your own for the first time or you're a newlywed embarking on married life and have to economize for the first year. Whichever the case, you have only one room in which to live, and it must not only be attractive, convenient, and comfortable, but must meet all of your basic living needs as well.

A studio apartment is not merely a bedroom but a place where you dress, eat, relax, and entertain on a round-the-clock basis. Obviously, it must function well for all of these activities if it is to be a home that lives up to its potential. It may seem like a large order to cater to all of these activities within four walls, but decorating a studio apartment need not be difficult if you follow some basic rules that will make your task much easier and enable you to get the most out of available space. There is also another important consideration: The room should express your tastes, interests, and personality—as well as those of your spouse if you are married. Here are some guidelines to help you create a warm and comfortable environment within those four walls, one that says something about you and whoever else lives there.

PLANNING AND PLACEMENT

Nowhere is planning as vital as it is in a studio apartment. A sound plan for the room and correct placement of furniture within it can spell the difference between order and chaos. The most practical way to plan your one-room apartment is to do it on paper first. Measure the room carefully and draw its outline on graph paper, using the scale of one-half inch being equal to one foot or, if you prefer, one-quarter inch being equal to one foot. Alternatively, you can let the squares act as a measuring guide. Your next step is to buy templates of furniture shapes from an art store, which are available in the same measurements of inches per foot. Cut these out and move them around on the graph paper plan until you have created a good arrangement that meets your living needs and allows for convenient traffic patterns. Remember, it is infinitely easier to arrange furniture on paper than hauling it around physically; the plan indicates how much you can include for comfort and also acts as a shopping guide.

As you arrange your furniture in this way, bear in mind the following two points: convenience and good looks. When furniture is correctly grouped, you can move from activity to activity without tripping over things. If the furniture fits well together and pieces seem made for each other, you will produce overall good looks. Try out lots of different groupings until you find the one you like the most.

The ideal room is hard to find. Many studios are small and confined, squared off and uninteresting, or long and narrow. Others might have a door that opens the wrong way, an awkwardly placed window, or other architectural elements that seem to preclude the perfect layout. However, all these problems can be dealt with and sometimes they lead to good solutions that add to the character of the room.

If you plan for convenience you'll make living all the more comfortable in your one-room apartment. For instance, items for certain activities should be grouped together. A bookcase should be handy to a desk, dressers near a closet or bathroom, and dining furniture within easy reach of the kitchen. In the same vein, a reading light should be adjacent to an easy chair or other types of seating, china and linen storage handy to table and bed, and record storage part of an entertainment center.

If a room is to be really efficient, traffic patterns should work correctly for the best results. If possible, the pathways in your room should be as direct as you can make them, so that you don't have to walk around furniture or squeeze between pieces.

Be certain you have easy access to windows and doors of closets. There is nothing more irritating on a day-to-day basis than windows you can't reach, doors that are obstructed, or chairs that bump into other items.

Once you have taken care of convenience, it is vital to consider the overall appearance of the room. A well-balanced arrangement of furniture makes any room appear settled and orderly. A haphazard grouping introduces a feeling of disorder and messiness.

When arranging your furniture, always begin with the larger pieces and build around them. However, avoid a grouping that puts all the bulky pieces at one end and therefore makes the room look empty and unfinished in other areas. When this is the only feasible arrangement, balance the weighty end with collections of pictures or shelves on the opposite wall.

It is vital that you always bear in mind the scale of the room. Furniture should be of the correct scale to suit the room's dimensions, neither too small nor too large. For example, a large chest or armoire will make a tiny room seem much smaller; on the other hand, several small pieces in a large room will not only look lost but will create a barren feeling as well. For these reasons, limit the furniture to what you really need and what the room can comfortably hold. A few well-chosen pieces in a small room create a neat, uncluttered look. A large room will benefit from extra furniture and accessories to fill in odd corners and counteract bare spots.

FURNITURE: THE BASIC ESSENTIALS

Since you are catering to many living needs in a studio apartment, you must select your furniture with great care. Apart from determining the function of a room, furniture is generally the focus of a decorating scheme. It is the longest lasting in terms of the investment you are making, as well as the most important from the point of view of comfort. Before making any purchases, consider both your present and future needs to avoid making any costly mistakes. Select well-made, sturdy items that will wear well for a number of years even if these are more expensive than others you might see. It's worth it in the long run.

Beds and other furniture for sleeping are your first consideration. More than ever before, you now have a remarkably wide range to choose from. In terms of appearance and the best utilization of space, select a piece of furniture for sleeping that also doubles as seating. The *sofa bed* is ideal for this purpose. Available in practically every size, shape, and style, it can be upholstered in a variety of different fabrics. Most do not betray their dual purpose. When the seat cushions are removed, the bed folds out of the sofa; thanks to improved engineering, this task is now simple to perform. You can get a love seat-size sofa bed that opens up into a single bed or others that become queen- and king-size beds. Providing total seating and sleeping comfort, they are well worth the extra cost. As an alternative, you might consider the *daybed,* which is usually about thirty inches wide and so takes up less room than a normal bed. Sometimes the head and footboard are upholstered to match the mattress; you can add bolsters and pillows to create a sofa look. This works well against a wall, with lots of extra cushions added for comfort. It can also be used in the center of a room to provide seating from either side. The *storage* bed is a boon in a one-room apartment. It comes in a variety of designs and can be found in most furniture and department stores. A storage bed usually consists of a mattress placed on top of a wooden storage unit containing drawers or open shelves. If you are working on a budget, have the storage unit made by a carpenter to suit the room's dimensions and add your own mattress. Another practical idea when price is a consideration is the *single bed* made to look like a *divan.* To do this, simply have a fitted spread made to cover the bed down to the floor. Matching bolsters arranged at each end and across the back do the rest. For additional comfort, include a selection of throw pillows.

Your second consideration is *surface-area furniture.* This includes tables for dining, end and coffee tables, and desks. The *Parsons table* is undoubtedly the most versatile item and one of the best buys around. It comes in all types of woods, painted finishes, or covered with a plastic laminate, and it is entirely dual-purpose. It works as a desk or for dining. Because of its simplicity of design, it can be used in either a traditional or contemporary room. A simple *glass table* with chrome legs functions in the same manner; thanks to its see-through qualities it appears to take up less space. If you have enough space to include a standard *dining table,* look at the latest scaled-down pieces now available, which are specially made to fit into small areas. These come in period and modern designs and in a variety of wood tones. An alternative is the traditional *drop-leaf table,* which has the appearance of a console when the leaves are dropped and takes up little space. With the two leaves lifted it services four. Some styles come with extension leaves that can be added when more guests are being entertained. Similarily, you can utilize a drop-leaf table of modern design in the same manner. If a tight budget precludes any of these, have a *circular piece of unfinished wood* cut to the desired size, attach it to a metal tripod base, which should cost only a few dollars, and camouflage it with a floor-length cloth. This can be used as a surface for a lamp, magazines, books, and accessories when not needed for meals. Finally, if space is really at a premium, buy a circular or square *card table* that folds and can be stored in a closet. This is easy to set up for evening meals and its utilitarian looks can be hidden with a floor-length cloth. An alternative to the card table is a set of *stacking tables,* generally called snack tables, designed for individual use. These serve one person for buffet meals and can be set up next to seating pieces in the room. They easily can be stored in a corner or in a closet.

Coffee and *end tables* are a must for total comfort and convenience in a one-room studio. The coffee table is needed to service the seating arrangement; end tables are required for lamps and provide surface space for accessories. The size of the coffee table depends on the dimensions of the room and available floor space. Select a small-scale coffee table if the room is small, preferably one made of a light wood or glass and chrome, since these look best in confined space. In general, two end tables are required and should be positioned on either side of a bed to hold lamps. These are also available in a variety of wood tones, chrome and glass, plastic, plus painted wood finishes. If you simply don't have the space for two end tables, consider using a small *desk* on one side of the sleep-type furniture that will perform double duties. Or use a storage *chest* in place of an end table. *Cubes* with hinged tops work as coffee and end tables; the interior storage space they provide is a great asset. When your budget is tight, use two small *unfinished circular wood tables* topped with matching floor-length cloths.

A desk and a chest provide extra surface space. Even if space is limited, they can often be fitted into a scheme through clever placement. To repeat, either or both can double as end tables; the desk can often serve as a dining table, with the chest acting as a server. Scale and the materials used are vital; they should fit the dimensions of the room; the design should blend with the overall decorative scheme.

Your third consideration is *supplementary seating,* consisting of extra pieces that work in conjunction with the main seating piece, such as a sofa bed or divan. *Chairs* are an obvious choice; if possible, include at least one comfortable easy chair in your arrangement. If it comes with a matching *ottoman,* so much the better. Several ottomans can be used in place of chairs; since most models come on casters, they can easily be moved around at will. When space is really tight, you can resort to large *floor pillows.* These can be stacked in a corner or a closet—even under a bed—and need only be brought out when guests arrive. They are comfortable and decorative and take up much less space than a chair. *Stacking* or *folding chairs* are ideal for dining in a small space; they perform double-duty as auxiliary seating when a large crowd gathers. Yet another alternative are small upholstered *benches* or stools that can be grouped around a coffee table; these are definitely space savers. The canvas *director's chair* is a comfortable and convenient addition in a seating arrangement; when several are included, they can be used at the dining table as well.

Your fourth consideration is *storage space,* which is really a question of where you find it or can make room for it. However, many pieces of furniture are available that serve storage as well as other functions. A handsome *chest of drawers* is a lovely addition to a studio apartment; of course, it provides plenty of drawer space for all manner of items. However, when it is not possible to include a chest, use your ingenuity and adapt some of these ideas.

1. A low chest or trunk works as a coffee table in front of a bed and provides interior space for all manner of items. Cover an old trunk with fabric or a vinyl wall covering, revamp it with paint or lacquer, or top it with a large piece of glass to extend the surface space.

2. Buy a filing cabinet containing two drawers, top it with a piece of circular wood and add a floor-length cloth in a pretty fabric or one made of felt. The drawers can be used to store all manner of items, from records to nonseasonal clothes, and are easily accessible by just lifting the cloth. The whole works as an attractive end table next to a chair or sofa bed.

3. When the storage situation is really acute and space is scarce, go upward with storage furniture rather than out onto the floor. Bookshelves are ideal, since they can hold much more than just books. In fact, you need not house books in them at all. Buy decorative boxes or baskets and use them to house linens, nonseasonal clothes, records, papers—almost anything you wish to store. Be imaginative and arrange the baskets or boxes in attractive ways to add decorative touches to the room. The bookcases can go as high as the ceiling and can cover part or all of a wall if you so desire. They can be built in or freestanding. Étagères can be utilized in the same way.

4. Wall-hung furniture also saves floor space and provides lots of storage facilities. Look at the units that have both high and base storage cabinets intermingled with the shelves. The cabinets and cupboards hide a multitude of things that cannot be on view, while the open shelf space permits you to display personal items, plants, paintings, and all kinds of accessories. Some systems come with a drop-leaf table that works as a desk, a vanity, or a dining area.

5. If you need a work surface and more drawer space than the average desk contains, consider this do-it-yourself idea. Buy two double-drawer filing cabinets

in a bright color and use them as pedestals for a desk top made out of a large piece of wood. Paint this a matching color or cover it with a self-adhesive vinyl or plastic laminate. Position the filing cabinets against a wall and leave enough space between them for a chair or stool. You can use the filing cabinets to store a variety of items in addition to stationery and the like. You can also house a small mirror and cosmetics in one of the drawers, so that the unit doubles as a vanity.

6. Utilize the insides of closet doors for attaching shoe bags, plastic caddies for various items, and racks for belts, scarves, and ties. If there are shelves in the closet, triple their space by using decorative boxes or ones made of see-through plastic to store sweaters, lingerie, and the like. Stack the boxes to the ceiling if necessary. Don't forget the closet walls. Hooks can be added to hold many things.

There is no limit to storage possibilities, even in the tiniest of spaces. By using your ingenuity and imagination you can find a spot for everything you need in your one-room apartment.

Color Plays an Important Role

The color scheme of your one-room apartment is of major importance. You must select it carefully and be certain you can live with it on a round-the-clock basis. It must not become boring, overpowering, or depressing with constant viewing. Lastly, it must be suitable for the size of the room.

We all have color preferences. However, it is vital to consider the various effects color creates in a room. For example, dark, sunless rooms come alive and look infinitely more cheerful when washed with bright yellows, oranges, tones of pink from rose to coral, red, and some of the natural sand tones. By the same token, a room that is too sunny will look cooler when splashed throughout with blues, greens, white, and such deeper tones as gray and brown. The small room grows in size when the walls and ceiling are painted white or other pale tones. Large barnlike rooms appear more intimate and cozy when treated to deep or brightly colored walls. Bear all of these points in mind, select one or more colors that will produce the effect you desire, and then go ahead and develop the scheme. Because a room painted in one color would be boring, it's a good idea to choose a secondary or accent color. These are limitless; the second, maybe even third, color can be yet another of your favorites or one taken from a painting, a fabric, a wall covering, or a floor covering. A lovely harmonious effect can be created when you use this technique.

Walls painted a solid color are generally restful and are easy to live with and decorate with accessories. They also make the perfect backdrop for furniture because they are not competitive. Apart from this, they tend to stretch space by means of visual illusion because the eye is not stopped by contrasts. However, you may wish to cover your walls with a wall covering or fabric. If this is the case, you must pay special attention to the pattern and the number of colors it contains. Here are some points to bear in mind.

Large, dominant patterns advance and reduce the sense of space. Avoid them in small or medium-sized rooms; utilize them only in spacious surroundings.

Airy patterns such as trellis, lattice, and plaids help to open up a room and make the space appear larger. They work in almost any room.

Small-scale patterns look lost in a room of large dimensions. Utilize them for smaller or medium-sized rooms.

Stripes induce a feeling of height because they lead the eye up. They are ideal for use in rooms with low ceilings.

Abstracts and stylized patterns introduce a wholly contemporary feeling. They should be used only with modern furniture.

Documentary prints, toiles, chintzes, and florals tend to create a more traditional mood. They look their best when used as a background for period reproductions or antiques.

Bright or dark colors advance and make small areas seem smaller, busier, and more confined. Reserve them for a larger space.

Too many vibrant colors in one pattern produce a "noisy" feeling and soon become overpowering and hard to live with on a twenty-four-hour basis. Avoid them in a one-room apartment.

The floor covering you select introduces color and sometimes even pattern, depending on the type you have chosen. Here is a checklist of the different effects floor coverings create.

Wall-to-wall carpeting introduces a feeling of luxury, warmth, and comfort. It tends to make the floor area seem much larger, especially if it is in a solid color.

Patterned carpeting diminishes the feeling of space to such a limited degree that it is not worth dismissing if this is your preference. However, don't use a patterned carpet if there is a patterned wall covering on the walls. Instead, go for a solid color. Since a one-room apartment gets heavy traffic, select a good carpet that will take lots of wear and tear. Look at those made of man-made fibers, such as nylon, acrylic, polyester and the indoor/outdoor carpeting, which is extremely durable.

Area rugs can be utilized to demarcate areas of space for different activities within a one-room apartment. You can use several, depending on the actual size of the room. One will pinpoint the seating/conversation arrangement, another a desk/work area, a third the dining section. Always select an area rug in a color that blends with the overall scheme or one with a pattern that suits the style of the furniture. You can choose from orientals, Indian, Moroccan, American Indian, Greek flokatis, and many modern designs as well. The latter are often made of man-made fibers that are durable and easy to spot clean.

The plain wood floor can look handsome when it has been cleaned and refinished. It appears to increase the feeling of spaciousness in a room of any size. However, when left bare it looks—and is—cold, lacking comfort or soundproofing qualities. Area rugs are a must.

Vinyl tiles are hard-wearing and most resilient in a one-room apartment. They come in a lovely range of colors. All manner of interesting effects can be created through the use of different colored tiles arranged in a unique pattern. However, like a wood floor, vinyl tiles produce a cold feeling, are cold to walk on, provide little comfort, and do not offer any soundproofing. They should be supplemented with area rugs.

Whichever type of floor covering you select, remember that it has to last a number of years and must therefore be durable and easy to maintain in pristine condition. It must also please you visually and aesthetically.

Finishing Touches

Like any other type of apartment, a one-room studio needs a few finishing touches to make it look well furnished and complete. Lighting and accessories help accomplish this and must not be neglected in your overall plan.

Lighting, in particular, must be carefully thought out for a studio that serves a multitude of needs on a twenty-four-hour basis. The fixtures you select must provide the correct overall lighting, as well as proper illumination in specific areas. They must also introduce a mood that is restful and easy to live with. To do this the lighting must be positioned in strategic spots around the room for the correct distribution of light.

The ceiling fixture, positioned in the middle of a ceiling, is a common type of general lighting usually found in most apartments. It spreads light across the entire area and enables you to see throughout the room. However, it is often unattractive and generally does not create a specific mood. It is mostly operated by a switch near the front door and is useful to keep intact since it illuminates your entry into the apartment. You can improve the ceiling light by adding a new fixture, such as a handsome chandelier, or a shade, which diffuses and usually softens the light. Diffusing shades are translucent, generally white, and are made of glass, plastic, or paper. They are either attached to the bulb itself or affixed with screws to the metal rim of the ceiling fixture. Many interesting designs are available today.

A table lamp or other types of lamps should be used in conjunction with the ceiling fixture. When these are correctly shaded, they introduce additional soft, diffused light, helping to add to the mood of the room and enhancing its decorative overtones as well. Lamps placed on end tables located on either side of a seating/sleeping piece provide the correct illumination for reading, sewing, or general relaxation.

Floor lamps are ideal to use in a studio apartment since they don't take up surface space. They can be placed next to a chair, a dining area, or simply used to illuminate a dark corner. Designs come in both traditional and modern styles to suit any decorative mood. Many are handsome and well designed. Some even have the appearance of a piece of sculpture; when this is the case, they add to the good looks of the studio apartment.

Indirect lighting is perfect for introducing a restful mood because it does not give off harsh, direct rays that cause shadows. You can use a floor lamp with the light directed up to the ceiling for this effect. Or you might prefer valance lighting, which consists of fluorescent tubing that washes a wall or draperies with indirect light; it must always be concealed behind a valance, a cornice, or other shield.

Wall fixtures save surface space. They come in all styles and thus suit any decorative scheme. They can be attached to the wall on either side of a bed, near a desk or work area, or above the dining table.

Low-hanging ceiling fixtures, lamps, and wall lights should be used to create proper illumination in any area where a specific activity takes place. Be sure to include one of them on or close to a desk or a study/work/hobby corner as well as where you dine, read, or dress. In this way you will provide total comfort at all times, while adding to the mood of your twenty-four-hour room.

Accessories help to give life, color, and movement to a one-room apartment. They also say something about your tastes and so stamp an environment with your personality.

Because they add to the room's visual appearance, accessories must be selected with care and arranged with skill and imagination to obtain the best results. A word of warning: When they are pulled together in a somewhat haphazard fashion, they introduce a cluttered, messy look that detracts from the room's overall appearance. Also, don't include too many for the same reason. It is far better to select only a few items to create the effect you desire and store the remainder. After a few months you can change the accessories to introduce a new look.

Unadorned walls soon begin to look boring, particularly in a room that works around the clock. Hang prints, graphics, paintings, or family photographs in attractive arrangements; use a selection of china plates or wall plaques to introduce visual interest, color, and pattern.

Arrange collections of decorative objects on a tabletop, wall-hung shelves, a dresser, or a coffee table. Be sure they are illuminated so that they can be seen to best advantage.

Let books make a definitive statement about you in your one-room apartment. Arrange them on wall-hung shelves, built-ins, or freestanding pieces. Their colorful jackets add life to a wall. When accessories and plants are interspersed among the books, you create interesting wallscapes that are visually appealing and add a finished look to any room.

Rooms that are well accessorized seem to be much more alive than those that have a paucity of items. But only display those things you really like and be sure they blend perfectly with the room's furniture and the overall decorative scheme.

Vera.

PRECEDING PAGES Do-it-yourself plank paneling and the use of brilliant colors and unusual patterns can create an interesting effect without a large expenditure of money. Since the selection of pattern and fabric sets the basic mood, it's fun to try a vibrant print-on-print combination. There would be little expense involved in switching moods. It is simply a matter of changing the fabric panels and draperies and selecting new sheets. In this particular room a brilliant red carpet establishes the basic color scheme. A strikingly modern geometric fabric in red, white, and black with a touch of subtle pink is used to line the bed niche, frame the window, and is also repeated in the throw pillows. Lots of white in the casement and upholstery fabrics complete the lively scheme. Space is a vital concern in this tiny studio apartment. The biggest space saver is the old Murphy bed idea in a new form. The bed swings up into the fabric-lined niche and stows away behind paneling to which a large painting has been firmly attached so that it can be viewed when the bed is hidden. Small doors in the paneled wall next to the bed swing open to reveal a mini-bar and entertainment center that capitalizes on the degree of depth needed for the bed's niche. The low sofas, ottoman, and end tables are in scale with the size of the room. The tables also provide hidden storage space underneath their lift-off tops. The use of hanging lamps saves floor space that would normally be taken up by floor lamps. Easy-care surfaces help keep this small but functional apartment looking clean and neat.

OPPOSITE For this one-room home designer *Dom Loscalzo* used an American Indian theme that effectively combines traditional and contemporary moods. The unifying factor is the use of imitation wood beams to establish an overall effect and visually divide the available space into living and sleeping areas. The beams form a tepee design around the bed and provide extra interest on the walls and ceiling. The geometric patterns of triangles and sharp edges enhance the American Indian theme. By placing one floor-to-ceiling beam in the middle of the room and arranging the sofa with its back to the bed area, a separate sitting and entertaining area is formed. A walnut open-front bookcase serves storage and lighting needs and acts as a divider. A coffee table (not visible) doubles as a low dining table; four leather hassocks can be stored underneath the table and pulled out to provide additional seating. The bedspread's tribal motif, done in an evergreen ground with a white and orange pattern, sets the color scheme. The terra-cotta lamps, American Indian-motif throw pillows, wall sconces in traditional American Indian design, paintings, and glazed pitcher and bowl on the dresser echo the basic theme and complete the effect. The light orange paint on the ceiling, rich orange carpeting underfoot, and textured walls round out the use of color and cohesiveness necessary in a one-room apartment.

OVERLEAF This warm, attractive room looks more like a cozy sitting room/library than a one-room apartment—which is the secret of its success. During daytime hours the clean, neat look that is created through the effective use of a single handsome pattern and a soothing paint color sets the scene for a combination working living room/den/dining room. The rich gold walls take on a sunlit effect during the day and glow in warm light in the evening. The use of a dark blue small-scale pattern consisting of small flowers is easy on the eyes and not apt to become tiresome from day to day. The border motif, which uses the same colors and pattern in a slightly larger scale, frames the window and fireplace, thereby creating a unifying effect. A plaid fabric in the same sophisticated colors is used to cover the skirted table. It harmonizes with the predominant pattern yet visually creates a separate dining area. The dishes, plants, and baskets echo the subtle floral theme. Since effective use of space is critical in a one-room apartment, cleverly hidden storage space behind the curtains, under the skirted table, and inside the low stool are welcome pluses. The glass coffee table appears to take up no visual space and slides out of the way so that the sofa can easily be converted to a double-sized bed for comfortable sleeping. During the day the sofa bed is enlivened with the trim seat cushions and an array of matching throw pillows.

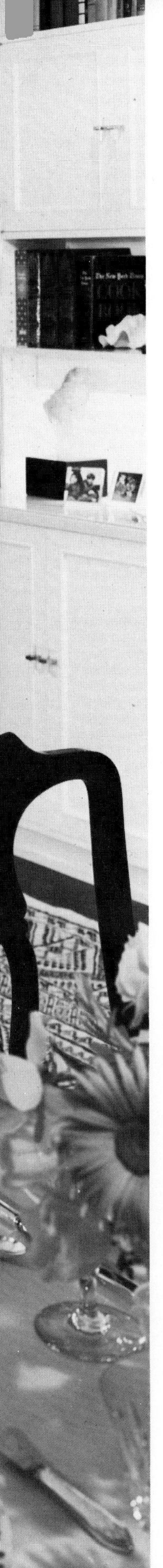

A one-room apartment must play many, many roles gracefully. Interior designer *Sue Morris* has made the most of this large rectangular space both decoratively and functionally. Clever space planning and a deft combination of dramatic patterns set off by great splashes of room-widening white do the trick. The Moroccan area rug, in a rich beige and brown, has a nondirectional pattern that separates the sitting/sleeping space from the dining area. The rich brown is repeated in the quilted ottoman and provides the background color of the Queen Anne white lace print on the sofa bed and wall covering, which can be seen near the window. The citrus color in the center of the flowers decorating the sofa and wall fabric is used as an accent color in the sofa cushions and the table lamp. The beige tone in the rug is repeated in the wicker coffee table/storage cube, which moves easily out of the way to make room for the bed when the sofa bed is opened. At the dining end of the room the white Parsons table, flanked by walnut Queen Anne chairs, repeats the chocolate and white theme. The floral arrangement, seat cushion fabric, and linen napkins echo the lemon accent. The use of two large plants alongside the sofa bed add another dimension of natural color that is repeated in the dragon pattern on the dinner plates. A desire for bright light during the day and darkness for sleeping comfort are easily satisfied by means of vertical blinds. They take up no visual space and hide the unattractive lines of old double-hung windows. On the adjacent wall a handsome white storage unit houses books, a stereo, and a TV. China and glass are hidden below in one part, while clothing, shoes, and handbags are stored in another section.

OVERLEAF The combination of a few furnishings that are both functional and good-looking, accented by the clever use of color and texture, can turn an attic with no natural light into a cheerful, bright, and practical studio apartment. The key to success in this room is the modular furniture grouping. The modular pieces, consisting of corner units, ottoman, and armless chairs, can be placed in any order and moved about to achieve different looks and meet different needs. A special hidden asset is the sofa end section, which opens up into a queen-sized bed. The Plexiglas coffee tables also serve multiple purposes. They can be spread around for casual entertaining or grouped together along a wall for buffet dining. Either way they appear to take up no visual space, which is an added plus in any small area. The simple color scheme also tends to increase the sense of space in this attic studio. The solid white background of walls, windows, and floor creates a unifying effect. The green, blue, and white awning-stripe fabric used for ceiling panels lends a sense of height to the sloped ceiling and establishes the color scheme. This is repeated in the chair covers and throw pillows. The natural oak table and bentwood chairs underscore the light, open feeling and are in scale with the other furnishings. The old wood candle holders add a touch of nostalgia to the modern mood. A simple change of fabric on the ceiling panes, seat cushions, and throw pillows would provide a totally new look for the basic white shell and could change the feeling from modern to traditional with a minimum amount of expense or effort.

The artistic legacy of ancient Egypt is the basis for this contemporary decorating scheme. The pattern seems as current today as it was in the heralded days of King Tutankhamen. Interior designer *Douglas Sackfield* establishes the decorative theme for this square-shaped studio apartment through the use of one boldly patterned fabric. He uses it on the sleep sofa, ottomans, curtains, and as a wall covering. A jeweled pectoral pattern, the fabric was inspired by an elaborate gold falcon pendant inlaid with lapis lazuli, turquoise, carnelian, and blue glass. It is the key element in this very neat and uncluttered decorative approach. At the same time, it provides the warmth and charm so vitally important in a multipurpose environment. The rich feeling that is achieved through the extensive use of fabric requires a simple shell to set it off; there can thus be no chance of jarring or competing elements. All the flat surfaces, including walls, ceiling, and floor, are done in a soft white that exactly matches the white of the fabric. Simple wood strips painted a rich turquoise and secured along the walls and windows at intervals provide a touch of color and lend architectural interest to the walls without competing with the fabric. A companion fabric consisting of a small-scale geometric design is used as a border around the top of the walls above the horizontal wood strips; it is picked up again in the luggage-rack coffee table, which has detailed carved feet reminiscent of work done in ancient Egypt. Rush woven baskets and bamboo desk bases reiterate the overall theme. Furniture placement allows for easy flow of traffic; a small kitchen (not visible) is near the desk, which doubles as a dining table. The large ottomans can be pulled up to provide seating and then slide back opposite the sofa for after-dinner conversation. At the opposite end of the room (not visible), an entire wall is decorated in the rich jeweled pectoral fabric. A series of built-in bookcases are open-backed so the fabric shows through. Glass shelves set into the bookcases house a collection of Egyptian and Middle Eastern vases, sculpture, and books. In the central bookcase a tall pyramid-shaped stand displays a dramatic bust of a young Egyptian boy who keeps watch over the entire room.

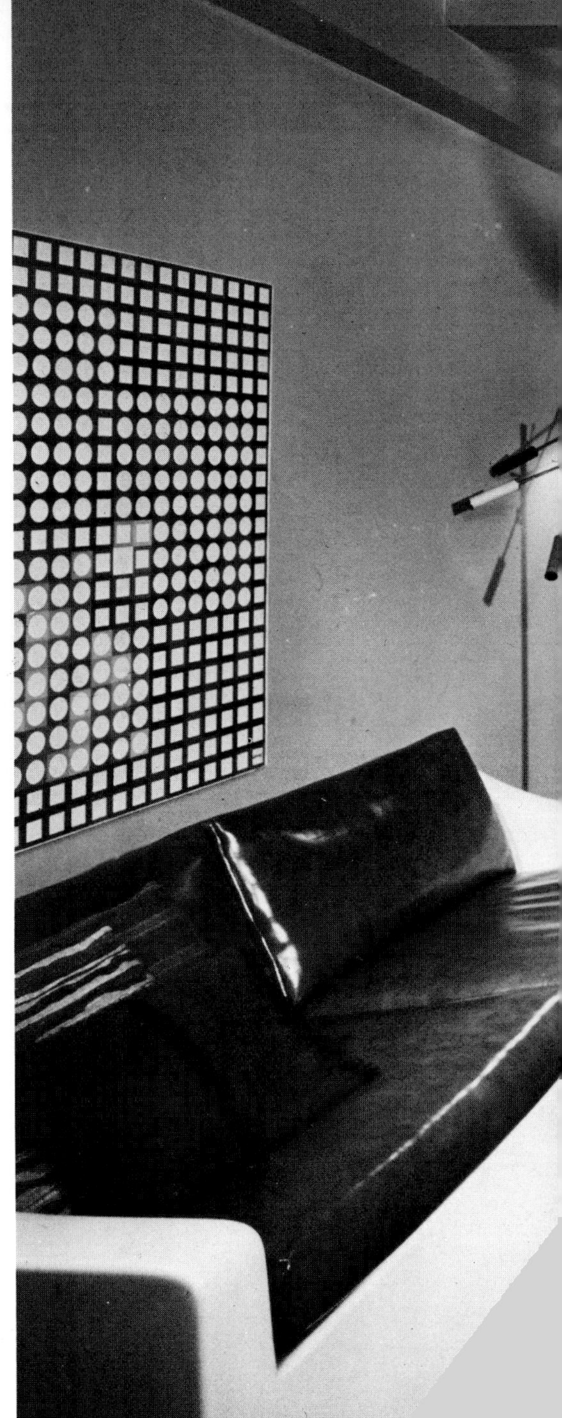

Designer *Susan Grant Lewin* created a casual environment on a budget in this studio apartment. In order to update an old-fashioned room and make it work around the clock, she combined tones of beige throughout to suggest structural changes without any actual remodeling. These soft colors are used on the walls and ceiling. Through the utilization of a monochromatic paint scheme the unattractive ceiling beams and old-fashioned radiator cover seem to disappear. The beige theme is repeated in the wicker chair and stools, in the chest that doubles as a coffee table, and in the light-finished wood of the wall-hung shelf arrangement. By using two pairs of shades hung reverse roll within their frames, the old-fashioned windows are deftly handled in a contemporary bare-bones fashion that works well with the other furnishings. The set that can be pulled down is broadly striped in cream and beige for horizontal decorative emphasis. The plain window shades, which are installed to roll from the bottom up, were chosen to filter out glare. The clever combination of shades provides a choice of easy day-and-night light control for the sofa bed and the desk. To make the most of available floor space in this narrow apartment, the furniture is placed along the walls. The only pieces that extend into the heavily trafficked area can easily be moved out of the way for a large buffet supper or disco dancing. At the far end of the apartment (not visible), a tiny dressing area provides space for a dresser and open shelves to store hats, shoes, and bags.

BAUHAUS

Artist-designer *Russ Elliot* has created four rooms in one through careful planning and deft do-it-yourself skills. The tiny apartment must play many roles on a twenty-four-hour basis for this work-at-home artist. It serves as an artist's studio the major part of the day, sleeping quarters at night, and is used for evening entertaining and three-meals-a-day dining. The selection of a dark brown color scheme works well in this small area. The brown wood paneling was put up in no time at all and the beams and wood valance were painted to match. The captain's beds, with artist-supply drawers in their bases, were also painted to match the walls and positioned to create a compact, L-shaped sleeping area. They also serve as daytime sofas and as banquettes when the room is used for dining. The desk/table (not visible) set across from the windows can be brought over to provide a dining surface. Mr. Elliot's own flower paintings stand out vividly against the dark walls and add a dash of color to the dark scheme. Ferns conceal the air conditioner when it is not in use. The rest of the radiator cover is mirrored to serve as a display space for a shell and coral collection. The octagonal, earth-tone floor tiles add visual interest and are easy to maintain. All the surfaces are easy to care for, which is important in a round-the-clock environment, especially one that serves as an artist's studio during the day.

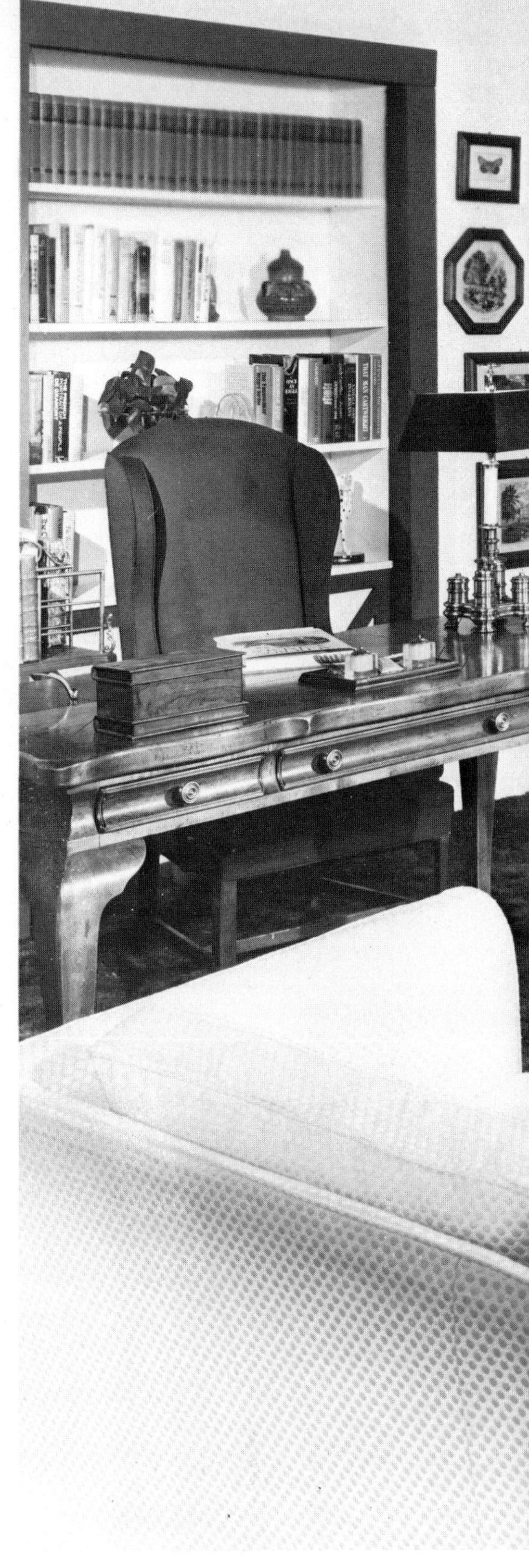

This handsome room, which looks like an elegant study, is actually a one-room apartment that serves a variety of living needs. Through sound planning, careful selection of furniture, and a good decorative scheme it provides the comfort and practicality usually found in several rooms. Designer *Mary Kay Baldwin* used carefully selected pieces of furniture and grouped them together for good looks, comfort, and convenience. To avoid a cluttered look, only a minimum of pieces are used, and these essential pieces create a handsome effect. The sofa, which converts into a bed, is serviced by a steel-and-glass coffee table. The desk in front of the recessed bookshelves works as a dining surface when required; stacking chairs housed in a closet provide seating. In addition, the wing chair behind the desk can be pulled into the seating area when needed. Such items as the tall étagère, books, accessories, and a collection of old prints add visual interest. At night the coffee table is simply moved to one side to serve as a night table when the sofa is opened up. Storage chests (not visible) line the wall facing the desk. The room draws its tranquil mood from a color scheme based on oyster, brown, and a mingling of blues ranging from reef to aquamarine. The reef blue is used for the textured fabric used to upholster the sofa bed; it is shown off to best advantage within a shell of palest aquamarine on the walls, ceiling, and the sheer curtains. The oyster and brown combination appears in the pinch-pleated tieback draperies and in the chair. The coffee-brown carpet, the warm glow of wood in the étagère and desk, and the lambrequin-style framework at the windows, which was painted brown, complete this soothing color scheme.

In a tiny studio apartment mix-and-match seating offers a multitude of arrangements that provide solutions to many living situations. In this contemporary, sleek one-room apartment the sleep sofa and stationary love seat provide comfortable living by day and sleep accommodations by night. To facilitate the change from daytime to sleeping needs, both the chrome-and-glass cocktail table and the ottomans have been equipped with casters. Both the sofa and love seat are of the same style; they are covered in an identical nubby flame-stitch pattern, producing a coordinated look and establishing a basic color scheme. The brick, putty, and white fabric makes a contemporary statement that is echoed in the cozy brick-colored floor, done in wall-to-wall carpet tiles with area rugs laid on top for added decorative interest. The mirrored panels and silver-tone horizontal blinds repeat the modern theme and add a sense of brightness at the same time, making the room look bigger. Storage space is critical in a small environment. In addition to being decorative, mirrored screens play yet another role. Behind the panels a dressing area and open shelves are hidden in a tiny odd-shaped alcove. Built-in bookcases, a low buffet, and end tables that flank the sofa provide additional storage space and surfaces to display artifacts gathered during vacations. The dining area (not visible), located at the opposite end of the room from the sleep sofa, has a glass-topped rectangular table that also doubles as an at-home work space. A grouping of hanging plants placed in front of the silver blinds adds a touch of color and provides decorative impact.

Simplicity is often the key to success in decorating a one-room apartment because it does not create the feeling of being overpowered by one's furnishings. Although this apartment is pared down to a few essentials, it retains a warm feeling through the use of interesting colors and textures. The basic evergreen, white, and beige color scheme is soothing and easy to live with. It works well for daytime and evening activities. Tatami, a traditional flooring material, is stapled to the walls and sprayed a deep evergreen. The effect is one of both intimacy and texture. The major piece of furniture, a luxurious full-sized sleep sofa, is upholstered down to its trim Parsons leg and generous roll arms so that no wood framing is allowed to show. The nubby white fabric adds another texture and is handsomely set off against the deep green walls. Theatrical gauze, which masks light without blocking it out entirely, is stretched on panels and hung at the windows. The panels are held on a sliding track so that different effects can be achieved by moving the panels to form various combinations. The panels cover the long wall entirely and hide two tall dressers that flank the windows and also provide space for storing clothing. The white vinyl floor is dramatic and easy to care for, which is important since it receives a lot of traffic. A narrow Parsons table placed behind the sofa serves as a display area for a collection of wicker and rock figures. Hanging bird-and-cricket cages at the windows are an interesting and inexpensive decorative idea that underscores the natural look. A low coffee table of natural wood (hardly recognizable as a commercial skid), bentwood dining chairs, small-scale tables, and a round dining table add the finishing touches to this tranquil studio apartment.

It is easy to establish a mood and period theme in decorating through the artful use of one dramatically strong fabric and furnishings reminiscent of a particular time. In this spacious one-room apartment designer *Douglas Sackfield* recreated a 1930s Art Deco atmosphere for a young artist. Although a fabric with a black background may seem a bit unusual, this eye-catching floral design certainly proves the point that success can be achieved through the clever use of one print. The strong statement the fabric makes means that there is little need for other decorative accessories. This actually eliminates the need for spending a big share of the budget on paintings and sculpture. The luxurious settee set at an angle to provide easy seating from either side is actually a daybed that features tufted seats, pleated roll arms, and end cushions all done up in the same fabric. The soft yellow leaves in the fabric are reflected in the pale yellow walls, which work well with the white tile floor. They provide a light shell that sets off the dark fabric effectively. Use of the same fabric on the sliding window panels, the folding screen, and the skirted ottomans eliminates the need for other wall window treatments that would either be too bland or too competitive if they were made of any other pattern or material. The floor-to-ceiling window panels slide away to reveal a magnificent view of the city by night. The folding screen hides the entrance to a corridor that houses a tiny old-fashioned bathroom and kitchen. Clever use of an oval mirror hung above the Art Deco-style Parsons table seems to widen the room. The brushed steel frame picks up the silvery sheen of the elegant period coffeepot, flower vase, and candlesticks. All the surfaces are easy to keep clean, which enhances the pleasure this apartment offers to both guests and owner.

NUTS
MINT

A Long Row of Candles
HIGH VALLEY

PRECEDING PAGES Since long hallways and corridors, which act as demarcating elements, are often absent in one-room apartments, designer *Shirley Regendahl* established a sensible relationship between the main area and the kitchen through use of similar color schemes. The living room wall covering sets the theme for the entire apartment. A rich interplay of springtime yellows, reds, oranges, and purple on a white ground provides the source for all the accent colors used throughout the carefully coordinated main room and kitchen. A canopied seating area is created from the studio bed. It is filled with an assortment of solid-color throw pillows that highlight the main colors in the fabric used to make a slipcover and the overhead canopy. By putting the daybed in the center of the room and placing it against the back of the long chest of drawers, a separate living area is established that is visually set apart from the dining end of the room. Also, this arrangement draws attention away from the long kitchen, which can be closed off by folding doors. A subtle secondary theme that harmonizes with the floral atmosphere is evident in the use of bamboo accents on the wood of the dining table, chairs, and tall chests, as well as in the brass coffee table and head and footboard of the sofa bed. Effective use of geraniums and anemones provides a live, three-dimensional accent for the vibrant mood that prevails throughout.

The vivacious color scheme in the long kitchen harmonizes with the colors used in the main room. The same citron tone used on the seat covers of the dining chairs, is also repeated on the kitchen cabinets and the folding doors. A rich tangerine covers the walls and floor and is repeated in the vertically striped window shades. A lime-green counter top completes the citrus mood, which is coordinated with the floral theme of the living area.

OVERLEAF In this handsome, traditional studio interior designer *Everett Brown*, F.A.S.I.D., set a classically patterned print against the richly burnished wood tones of the walls and furniture. The inspiration for the color scheme was derived from the red oriental rug. The sofa fabric pattern, which is similar to the rug motif, works equally as well at the windows, where it is used for curtains, laminated shade, and matching valance. The use of two similar designs is an excellent example of the marriage of pattern on pattern. The inclusion of small-scale accessories and furnishings does not detract from the strong decorative statement or from the expansive view of a city below, which gracefully leads to the harbor and the sea beyond. The magnificent view seems to make the apartment extend beyond its actual physical boundaries. During the day and in the early evening the shades are left up to provide a "frame" for the outside world. At night they provide privacy and darkness for sleeping comfort. Although this elegant setting seems more like a library than a one-room apartment, it nevertheless must work around the clock. When the sofa is opened for sleeping, the pillows can be stacked neatly under the handsome desk. The latter can easily seat two for dinner in front of the commanding view. The sophisticated oriental theme is extended to the lacquer-red walls of the kitchen (not visible). The same fabric is used for a shower curtain in the enamel blue bathroom (also not visible). The rich lacquer-red and blue tones are repeated in the leather-bound volumes housed in the built-in library shelves and in the small-scale accessories.

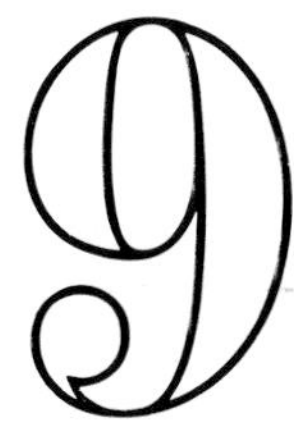

How to Create an Indoor Garden

Plants are an important decorating element, especially in city apartments, where the need for greenery and living things is most apparent. They add color, texture, shape, and life, do much to enhance furniture and furnishings, and in general help to round out the overall decorating scheme. These qualities apart, plants of all kinds help to introduce a finished look in a room that is sparsely furnished by filling in bare wall space and corners.

Practically every type of plant is available today. A large majority of these thrive in apartments provided they get proper care and sufficient light. Most stores and shops selling plants are happy to advise you about the correct choice of plant and the special care certain types need in your own special environment. It is important to pay attention to the plant expert so that you do not make costly mistakes or get disappointing results.

Armed with their specialized assistance, it is relatively easy to create your own indoor garden and so bring a touch of living greenery to your home. Here are some other useful guidelines to help you with your indoor gardening.

Plan the Garden

Before you make any purchases whatsoever, it is important that you plan your garden properly. Begin by examining the room where you intend to create the garden to assess the amount of space and light available. This will also help you decide on the kind of garden you are going to create (e.g., whether it will be large or small) and will suggest the type of plants you should use to obtain the best effect.

It is vital to select the right place for the garden. This might be in front of a window, near a door leading to a terrace, in a corner, against a stretch of bare wall, or at the edge of a dining area that adjoins a living room. But wherever it is, check the amount of natural light that flows into the particular spot and note the temperature of the room in general. These are important points to bear in mind, as all plants require a certain amount of light and the right temperature. Measure the area where you are going to create a garden regardless of whether this is a floor or window space. This information will help you to select the plants that are most suitable in terms of size and shape.

FOLIAGE PLANTS

Foliage plants are very popular. In the winter they suggest summer; in the summer they look cool and refreshing. They have year-round good looks, for, unlike flowering plants, they are never out of season and most can survive with less light. Here is a list of some favorite plants that do well in most apartments. They come in small and large sizes and can be used to create important effects in groupings on the floor or on low tables and benches.

1. Decora (*Ficus elastica*)
2. Rubber plant (*Ficus elastica*)
3. Fiddle-leaf fig (*Ficus lyrata*)
4. Bird's-nest fern (*Asplenium nidus*)
5. Schefflera actinophylla (*Brassaia actinophylla*)
6. Philodendron
7. Monstera (*Monstera deliciosa*)
8. Dracaena
9. Varied palms
10. Dieffenbachia

11. Cacti and succulents
12. Ferns of all types

Armed with this list, visit your local plant shop to view the plants and become acquainted with their colorations, textures, shapes, and sizes. Group several together to see the effect they will create before making a final choice.

If you are looking for smaller plants to include in the grouping of big, good-looking plants, consider the following, which can also be used in miniature gardens, on tabletops, or in window areas. All are small foliage plants with a dash of color such as pink, red, or yellow.

1. *Caladium hortulanum* (commonly called angel-wings, elephant's ear, or heart of Jesus)
2. *Saxifraga stolonifera* (commonly called mother-of-thousands)
3. *Coleus blumei* (commonly called flame nettle)
4. *Codiaeum variegatum pictum* (commonly called croton)
5. Begonias of various types

These plants can be combined with vining or trailing plants to create interesting effects, whether on shelves, in window areas, or on tabletops. Look for the following:

1. Pickaback (*Tolmiea menziesii*)
2. English ivy (*Hedera helix*)
3. Grapevine or grape ivy (*Cissus rhombifolia*)
4. Emerald feather (*Asparagus desiflorus "Sprengeri"*)

FLOWERING PLANTS

Flowering plants are popular because of the color they introduce into an indoor garden as well as their fragrance. Some flowering plants bloom seasonally while others bloom continuously. Most require a good amount of light. You might consider some of them to produce eye-catching effects in floor groupings, on shelves, surface areas, or windows, either alone or with foliage plants.

1. African violet (blooms all year)
2. Hyacinth & tulip (spring)
3. Gloxinia (spring and summer)

4. Geranium (blooms all year)
5. Amaryllis (Christmas)
6. Flowering begonia (blooms all year)
7. Azalea (spring and summer)
8. Daffodil (spring)

Types of Indoor Gardens

The type of indoor garden you create is dictated by the overall dimensions of the given room, the space you have available, the special effects you wish to produce, and the amount of money you have to spend.

A grouping of large, good-looking plants is highly dramatic and makes a strong, definitive statement in a room. The plants can be of varied types and heights. Taller ones can be grouped on the floor. Smaller plants can be included on low tables or stools, or tables of varying heights to create a well-balanced look. They should be contained in decorative pots that match or blend well to obtain the best visual result. Any of the foilage plants mentioned earlier can be mingled together to create a really stunning indoor garden. When grouping plants, turn them slowly so that you position them in the best way for real visual impact.

Small foliage plants, vining, and creeping plants, together with flowering plants can all be mingled in a window area to enhance a room. They can be grouped on a window ledge, on glass shelves fitted across the actual window, or in a unit built around the window ledge for this purpose. Group the plants carefully, paying attention to different textures and colorations, so that you produce the most attractive visual effects.

All of the above plants and any number of different types of ferns can be hung from the ceiling to introduce growing greenery into a room short on floor space. For the best visual results, suspend the plants at various levels to create a sense of movement. Utilize attractive baskets or containers. Hanging plants look especially effective when they are placed in front of a window, but they can be hung in other areas of a room. If you want to produce a woodsy, bowerlike feeling, use ceiling-hung plants in combination with a large floor grouping.

It is relatively simple to create a garden room by using a profusion of plants of all types, sizes, and shapes throughout. The results are both dramatic and refreshing. If this is the effect you want to achieve, select plants carefully, paying attention to coloration, texture, shape of leaves, and height. Group them with skill and imagination to show them off correctly, and, at the same time, to produce a balanced look in the room. Apartments with lots of windows are ideal for creating a garden room, as will become evident later in this chapter.

Lighting Effects

Daylight is important for a plant's growth. Artificial lighting is also necessary if you want to show off your plants to best advantage. This is particularly true if you have created a large floor arrangement of oversized foliage plants. Apart from this, artificial lighting is also important for plant maintenance and growth in most apartments.

All manner of lighting fixtures now on the market are specifically designed for use with plants in indoor gardens. These are usually spotlights that focus attention on the plants. They can either be placed on the floor among the plants or attached to a wall or ceiling. Whichever type of spotlight you use, be sure the light is directed at the plants at an angle to create interesting light-and-shadow effects on the walls and ceiling. The light can be directed from behind or up or down, depending on the special effects you wish to introduce into the room.

Similarly, small spots can be used on bookshelves or other types of units where plants are being displayed. Again, this type of lighting helps the plants to be seen to best advantage; an interesting interplay of light and shadow usually results.

A spherical lighting fixture that positions on the floor throws out incandescent light and looks marvelous when included in a floor garden of medium or large size. Some of the low oriental lighting fixtures that come in different shapes and sizes also work well. You can produce dramatic and striking results with a little experimentation.

For parties, mingle small votive candles in sturdy containers among your plants to create magical effects. Be sure the containers are placed at strategic points so that the candles do not singe the plants.

Plants and Accessories

Finally, consider arranging special accessories alongside or among your plants to introduce additional decorative overtones in a room.

If you have created a relatively large floor grouping of imposing-looking plants, choose equally important objects to mix in with them. This might include a stone garden statue, a stone birdbath, a ceramic animal, or a metal bird such as a crane or flamingo. Be certain the size of the object is correct for the scale of the plants and the overall garden area; otherwise the accessory will look lost.

A window garden gains in decorative impact when you include a few accessories along with the plants. By necessity, these must be fairly small objects to balance the smaller types of plants used.

China ornaments, crystal, and silver pieces all look beautiful on shelves that extend across a window with light streaming in. A variety of other objects can be placed on window ledges or units surrounding the window. These might include lacquered boxes, native handicrafts picked up during travels, pieces of Bristol glass, or papier-mâché animals from Mexico. However, if you have used flowering or foilage plants with a tinge of color, be sure the colors of the accessories blend in. Similar effects can be introduced on bookshelves and other surfaces where you have created an indoor garden through the inclusion of just the right decorative objects.

The outdoor mood can be emphasized in a garden room through the use of large pieces of sculpture or garden ornaments. Their size and exact placement is vital if they are to be shown off to best advantage and not appear dwarfed or overpowered by the profusion of plants. The sculpture or other items can either rest on the floor or can be placed on pedestals made of Plexiglas or white-lacquered wood. A large ceramic animal or a metal bird are both appropriate, helping to whimsically underscore the outdoor ambience.

Making an indoor garden is fun, providing a challenge to one's imagination and ingenuity. Whatever type you create, always be certain that it adds to the overall decorative look of the room. For, like all the other elements discussed in this book, it must help to produce a pleasing environment for apartment living —for all members of the family.

OVERLEAF One good way to expand a room and bring the outdoors inside is to create a greenhouse effect. This can brighten a room and broaden its horizons as well, as illustrated in this living room located in a basement apartment of a reconverted brownstone. The sloping windows had already been installed by the previous owners when the brownstone was remodeled. It was this area that gave the new tenants the basic idea. However, this same greenhouse look can be created in front of any large expanse of window if there is sufficient floor space. To demarcate the greenhouse/dining area from the living section a platform was built and covered with the same bright green carpet used in the living section. This new type of indoor/outdoor carpet has the look of grass. It is easy to clean with water or simply by vacuuming, is impervious to mildew or rot, and thus is ideal for the greenhouse ambience. To create a sense of total coordination, it was carried up over the front of the built-in unit that runs under the window and was topped with white-painted wood. Here all manner of small plants abound, backed up by others suspended in front of the windows and grouped on the floor. To completely fulfill the mood, a lush arrangement of plants was used on the étagère, while other large potted plants were scattered around the entire room. All were chosen for their scale, shape, and texture. Flowering plants add that extra splash of bright color. The green and white color scheme of the basic shell is punctuated by two fabrics in green and white splashed with yellow. One is a large-scale floral design, the other an airy abstract. Both are made of cotton and are cleverly coordinated for a harmonious effect. To further develop the outdoor feeling of the room a bamboo sectional sofa and étagère plus matching coffee table were selected for the living area. Wicker chairs partner a skirted table on the dining platform at the greenhouse end of the room. Like the carpeting, all these furnishings are durable and easy to keep in pristine condition.

A unique window treatment can be created with plants and special fluorescent lights, as illustrated here. Plants have been arranged at two different levels to curtain the large window, while fluorescent lighting built into the cove-type treatment assures good growth for the plants and focuses interest on them as well. The cove effect adds decorative flair to the area. It can be duplicated over a weekend by an inveterate do-it-yourselfer. As you can see, the window wall becomes a focal point, creating a lively and unique backdrop for other furnishings. Growing plants should always be grouped with an eye toward color, shape, and texture, as was done here. Pots can be of different types or uniform in design, depending on the decorative effect you wish to create.

This "blooming" window treatment introduces a fresh garden feeling at one end of a living room. It also adds a sense of balance to the off-center double-hung windows by making their awkward placement look less apparent. Artist-designer *Russ Elliot* pulled the textured window shade down on a dull view and set up his own garden inside. The translucent shade controls light falling on the greenery and is artfully decorated with rows of braid to echo the room's daffodil, spring green, and white color scheme. Above the window a Plexiglas valance, which was hand-painted by the artist-designer to simulate Tiffany glass, underscores the garden motif. A long, low wooden unit was built under the windows to conceal an unsightly radiator, unify the two windows, and create a spot for the miniature garden. Here a collection of small potted plants are well displayed together with accessories. The window garden is supplemented by three ceiling-hung pots of ivy, a tall palm, and a large fern placed on the floor beside the palm. This cleverly grouped combination introduces a lush green effect and gives the area extra decorative importance within the room. A mirrored, built-in bar with interior lighting adds a shimmering quality and reflects the growing greenery. Fulfilling the outdoor ambience are white director's chairs and a black garden table intended for drinks or snacks.

INDIAN
ARTS & CRAFTS

SONY

PRECEDING PAGES Windows are the logical place for plants in any apartment, but they are not always large enough to house a sufficient number of plants to create a dramatic or handsome effect. The solution is to build a window unit like the one shown here. The owners of this roomy city apartment built a base unit under the window, extending it along the entire wall. In addition to concealing an ugly radiator, recessed niches provide extra space for books and accessories. Bookshelves were added at each end (only one is visible); they flank the window, giving extra importance to the total wall. Potted plants were then grouped on the wide shelf, housed in a variety of old containers and baskets. Others were ceiling-hung to add to the lush effect. The entire treatment gives this end of the room added decorative impact. Of course, the window wall is the focal point of the room, a mass of living greenery and colorful accessories. A gaily patterned area rug pulls together the seating arrangement and effectively directs the eye toward the window wall.

When it is not possible to build a unit around a window, consider creating one somewhere else in a room to act as a display center for houseplants. That is the technique *Abbey Darer* used in this living room intended for a young couple. The designer added three tall and narrow floor-to-ceiling cupboards along the main wall to provide much-needed storage space for such things as a stereo, records, and a variety of other items. She then painted the two open sections between the three cupboards stark white and added an opaque plastic panel at the back of each to conceal lighting. Glass shelves were the final addition; they house all manner of small plants, including some of the vining or trailing variety. The back-lighted panel provides light and nourishment for the plants and helps to focus attention on them. They add a cool, summery look to the basic red and white shell, where a tree-patterned wall covering underscores the garden mood. The built-in for the plants provides extra visual interest in an otherwise ordinary and architecturally dull room.

VOLUME TWO
THE
THINGS
WORK

Windows on three walls are major features of this living room, located in a modern apartment in a high-rise building. They inspired interior designer *Jane Victor*, A.S.I.D., to transform it into a full-fledged garden room that is restful and refreshing in every kind of weather and in any season. She began by lining the floor with black and white tiles arranged to create the effect on an area rug. The ceiling was painted white and the windows were treated to narrow-slatted blinds in a silvery tone. Banquettes covered in a striking black and white print were grouped to form an expansive U-shape; they provide comfortable seating in the casual, easy-care room. The banquettes are serviced by three white marble coffee cubes, while a fourth glass-and-brass table serves as a handy bar. A profusion of plants are ranged around the floor in groups and singly; some are also suspended from the ceiling. They introduce a bowerlike effect and give the room its basic character.

A small window at one end of a living room in a converted brownstone apartment looked out onto an unattractive view. A profusion of plants was utilized to hide this view and eliminate the need for a window treatment. A "jungle" feeling was created through the use of varied types of foliage plants selected for their different shapes and sizes. They were arranged on the floor and on the window ledge; one was hung at the top of the window to create a feeling of movement and to balance the whole. Note how the plants echo the natural theme of the decor, produced by the brick wall, baskets, shells, African tribal artifacts, and the rattan sides of the recliners. Additional plants bring extra touches of greenery and textural play to the brick wall, which is also enlivened by books on suspended shelves.

The current trend toward natural themes in home furnishings is beautifully reflected in this environmental setting designed by *Emy Leeser*. A thicket of plants easily coexists with such furnishings as a butcher block table and leather-cushioned country-style benches; the luxurious sculptured carpet in a garden-green hue also helps to underscore an outdoor atmosphere. The designer let the brick wall of a facing building serve as a backdrop for her "curtain" of small plants, which are hung along the window wall and arranged on the sill. She balanced the window greenery with a tray garden filled with a collection of good-looking foliage plants of various types and sizes. The pebbles and shells that line the tray are more decorative than the gravel normally used for tray gardens of this type. Above the floor grouping a wall-hung unit displays smaller plants most effectively and adds to the overall look at this end of the living room. Antique English and oriental planters, terra-cotta pots, and straw baskets combine with the pebbles and shells in the tray garden and the flora and wall prints to bring nature indoors.

Bay windows, picture windows, and window walls are dramatic settings for flowers and plants because the natural light enhances their appearance; plants silhouetted against a window make interesting pictures. This room, which opens off a living room in a ground-floor apartment, has large windows on two sides. The owners decided to transform it into a garden room that works the year round. The ideas shown can be adapted to any room in any kind of apartment provided it has similar window walls. The room was lined with white wood paneling on two walls. The floor was covered with large-scale ceramic tiles in a textured white pattern. A foot-high curb made of plywood and covered with tile was run around the window walls and positioned a few feet from the glass. This trough makes marvelous planting beds of peat moss into which potted plants are placed and changed as often as desired. Here an exciting combination of plants of various types have been selected for their textures, shapes, and sizes. They mingle together in the beds, reinforced by hanging plants in one area of the side window. Along the opposite wall lucite shelves display a collection of seashells. While the plants provide the main color, the white paneling, floor tiles, and rattan furniture are complemented by the muted green, yellow, and pink print on the seat cushions and upholstered ottomans. Incandescent lighting is concealed behind wood valances above the window walls.

Index

CREDITS

Photo courtesy of Schweiger Industries, Inc., pages 14–15
Photo courtesy of Schweiger Industries, Inc., pages 24–25
Photo courtesy of Everett Brown, F.A.S.I.D., pages 22–23
Photo courtesy of Bloomcraft, Inc., pages 38–39
Photo courtesy of Collins & Aikman Corp., pages 58–59
Photo courtesy of Du Pont Company, pages 54–55
Photo courtesy of Congoleum Corporation, pages 68–69
Photo courtesy of the Belgian Linen Association, pages 72–73
Photo courtesy of the Belgian Linen Association, pages 74–75
Photo courtesy of the Belgian Linen Association, pages 92–93
Photo courtesy of Holmegaard of Copenhagen, pages 96–97
Photo courtesy of Collins & Aikman Corp., pages 110–11
Photo courtesy of Royal Copenhagen Porcelain and Royal Systems, Inc., pages 108–9
Photo courtesy of Levolor, Inc., pages 136–37
Photo courtesy of Angelo Donghia, A.S.I.D., pages 144–45
Photo courtesy of Collins & Aikman Corp., pages 148–49
Photo courtesy of J. Josephson, Inc., pages 152–53
Photo courtesy of Breneman, Inc., pages 170–71
Photo courtesy of Albert Van Luit & Co., pages 180–81
Photo courtesy of Eastman Kodel, pages 182–83
Photo courtesy of Eastman Kodak Company, pages 186–87